AF703972

Money AND Liberty

Money AND Liberty

How the Framers' Obsession with Protecting Your Money Shaped the Constitution

Rick Lynch

Copyright © 2025 Rick Lynch

All rights reserved. No part of this publication may be reproduced, distributed, or transmitted in any form or by any means, including photocopying, recording, or other electronic or mechanical methods, without the prior written permission of the publisher, except in the case of brief quotations embodied in critical reviews and certain other noncommercial uses permitted by copyright law. For permission requests, write to the publisher, addressed "Attention: Permissions Coordinator," at the address below.

Van Cortlandt Books
info@rick-lynch.com

ISBN: 979-8-9990448-0-8 (paperback)
ISBN: 979-8-9990448-1-5 (ebook)
ISBN: 979-8-9990448-2-2 (hardcover)

Printed in Purcellville, VA, U.S.A.

Library of Congress Control Number: 2025912385

Ordering Information:
Special discounts are available on quantity purchases by corporations, associations, and others. For details, contact info@rick-lynch.com

Publisher's Cataloging-in-Publication Data
Names: Lynch, Rick, 1964- .
Title: Money and liberty : how the framers' obsession with protecting your money shaped the Constitution / Rick Lynch.
Description: Purcellville, VA : Van Cortlandt Books, 2025. | Includes bibliographic references. | Summary: A study of Constitutional philosophy and history, specifically property rights, the paper money crisis, and the reasons the Bill of Rights was not included in the original Constitution. Uses the approach of revisiting forgotten Constitutional doctrine.
Identifiers: LCCN 2025912385 | ISBN 9798999044822 (hardcover) | ISBN 9798999044808 (pbk.) | ISBN 9798999044815 (ebook)
Subjects: LCSH: Constitutional history – United States. | Political science – Philosophy. | Political science – United States – History. | United States – Politics and government. | BISAC: POLITICAL SCIENCE / Constitutions. | POLITICAL SCIENCE / Political Ideologies / Democracy. | HISTORY / United States / Revolutionary Period (1775-1800).
Classification: LCC KF4541.L96 2025 | DDC 342.73--dc23
LC record available at https://lccn.loc.gov/2025912385

The great art of law-giving consists in balancing the poor against the rich.

-John Adams

Take mankind in general, they are vicious.... One great error is, that we suppose mankind more honest than they are.

— Alexander Hamilton

I am more and more convinced that Man is a dangerous creature, and that power whether vested in many or a few is ever grasping, and like the grave cries give, give.

— Abigail Adams

Table of Contents

Introduction

ALMOST NOBODY TODAY understands the U.S. Constitution. Revered by hundreds of millions the world over as a near-sacred totem and the embodiment of liberty and freedom, its intellectual foundations are as unknown to Americans as those of the Achaean League or the Amphictyonic confederacy.

To illustrate this lack of constitutional insight, we will consider a few very basic questions, the answers to which are vital if you are to understand the Constitution.

Question One

Why did the Framers refuse to put a bill of rights into the Constitution, saying such a move would be "unnecessary," "preposterous," and even "dangerous"?[1] If you cannot answer this question, you will never understand the most important part of the Constitution—the system of protections the Framers preferred over the Bill of Rights, the system of protections that they wrote into the original, unamended Constitution.

I go further, and affirm, that bills of rights, in the sense and to the extent they are contended for, are not only unnecessary in the proposed constitution, but would even be dangerous.

— Alexander Hamilton[2]

It may be that every American "knows" that the Framers gave us a bill of rights as a guarantor of various liberties (indeed, this idea is probably the most thoroughly ingrained in our collective psyche and national identity of ***all*** our founding beliefs), but the plain, historical, and undeniable fact of the matter is the Framers overwhelmingly ***rejected*** any notion of a bill of rights.

Fifty-five men, representing 12 states, attended the Convention. When a bill of rights was proposed, ***only three*** spoke in favor of the measure. The state delegations, voting in blocks, were ***unanimous*** in their rejection of the proposal.

This, of course, is why the Bill makes up the first 10 amendments to the Constitution and is not a part of the original document to come out of Philadelphia.

The Bill of Rights was ratified three and one-half years after the Constitution was ratified and was written by a different group of men, in a different city, in an entirely different state, and in a different political forum.

The Bill faced an even more hostile reception in the First Congress. Robert Goldwin notes in his book *From Parchment to Power* that the House was "almost unanimously opposed" to the Bill. This disdain for the idea was communicated to the Bill's sponsor "in terms that were caustic, scornful, and even derisive."[3]

Even the Bill's sponsor was opposed to the idea. He knew, however, that the Anti-Federalists would almost certainly end his political career if he did not push the Bill forward.

But ***why*** were the Framers so adamantly opposed to the Bill? This is vastly more important than the simple fact that they did indeed reject the Bill.

That's an easy question to answer. The Framers predicted, with perfect accuracy, that the Bill would not protect or ensure our rights, but would ***rob*** us of those rights. If you want to know what could possibly be dangerous about enshrining in law a list of rights that the Framers actually believed in, and believed in passionately, then see chapter 1.

On a happy sidenote, it turns out that knowing why the Framers rejected a bill of rights will tell you ***every single thing*** you need to know to demolish—utterly, completely, and finally—the ridiculous notion that the Second Amendment reads, in effect, "Militias are acceptable, and federal gun control is constitutional."

I promise you three things about this rebuttal to that argument:

1. You've not heard it before,
2. It does not rely on anything so damnably boring and esoteric as understanding 14th-century English common law

or the precise definition of "militia" as it evolved from the Anglo-Saxon tradition, and

3. It does, truly and honestly, ***end*** the debate about what the Second Amendment means.

Question Two

What rights were the Framers most concerned about and determined to protect?

Again, a very basic question. And if you don't know the answer, you cannot understand the Constitution. Conventional wisdom would point to the Bill of Rights to answer this question and would say, "Here is what the Framers most wanted to protect. Here is what was most important to them."

Wrong.

It may be hard to believe, but the Framers were obsessed with—and wrote the Constitution to protect—a right that you have never heard of. The Framers placed infinitely more value on this right than they did any of the constitutional rights we've all heard so much about for all of our lives.

They placed more value on this right than on your speech, religion, gun, and press rights. More value on it than that stuff about not quartering troops in your house, due process, search and seizure, grand juries, double jeopardy, self-incrimination, etc., etc., etc.

Could that possibly be true, you ask? Surely it is ridiculous hyperbole to say that in this rights-obsessed nation of ours, the right the

Framers valued above all others is one that virtually no American has ever even heard of. But it is true.

As one author noted, the Framers viewed this right with "an almost religious respect."[4] You will see very shortly that there was absolutely ***nothing*** "almost" about it, and that's why the Framers nearly always wrote of this right with frankly religious intensity.

John Adams wrote with, ahem, frankly religious intensity, that this right was as "sacred as the laws of God."[5] One delegate to the Convention said government power to oppress this right was (frankly religious intensity alert) "as alarming as the mark of the Beast in Revelation."[6]

This single right was written of in the Federalist Papers ***more than 17 times as often*** as the big three First Amendment rights ***combined***.

As another author wrote, this was a right so cherished by the Framers that all but four of those 55 men placed its protection behind only life and liberty in order of importance. And of the four who differed on this, three of them actually "put [its] protection ***ahead*** of liberty as the main object of society."[7]

I'll go further—not only is this the most important of rights, but it is the one most likely to be sacrificed in a representative government such as ours, and the entire Constitution was therefore constructed to protect this right.

Chapter 2 has all the details.

Question Three

Why do we even have a Constitution? Why did it come into existence? Just what, exactly, prompted the calling of the Convention that gave birth to it? You can't get more basic than this, and yet virtually ***no*** Americans know the answer.

The conventional and rather boring answer is that the British were gone and it was obviously time to create a new government to take the place of the old. Of course the principles and substance of this new government would be entirely opposite of those of the recently defeated monarchy. A reliance on the people, the common man, democracy, majority rule, and the vote were to bring liberty where before there had been tyranny. This conventional view is false on all counts.

As chapter 3 details, the Constitution came into being not because of ***anything*** to do with the departure of the British, but because the existing U.S. government, which had been in effect for nearly ***six years*** after the final British defeat at Yorktown, was failing in its primary duty of protecting its citizens from tyranny and oppression.

Why was it failing? Well, principally because of an overreliance on the people, the common man, democracy, and majority rule. As one Convention delegate said, "The evils we experience flow from the excess of democracy."[8]

The U.S. Constitution was created for no reason other than the failings of democracy in several of the newly independent states.

In fact, majority factions in several states were using the power of democracy to oppress, in a very specific way, a very specific and unpopular minority group. Who was this group? What was being done to them? We'll leave the "who" of it alone for the moment, but as for what was being done to them, they were being robbed of that unknown right mentioned above. ***Yes, it is true—the Framers of the Constitution overthrew the Articles of Confederation and created a new national charter to protect a right that you have never heard of.***

In the succeeding chapters, we will examine the Framers' views on these subjects, show how we have departed from constitutional doctrine, and tally up all that we have lost.

CHAPTER ONE

The Bill of Rights

"NOT ONLY UNNECESSARY, BUT PREPOSTEROUS AND DANGEROUS"[9]

> It remains astonishing that the great majority of the delegates to the Convention thought a Bill of Rights not merely unnecessary, but unwarranted, and they refused to put one into the Constitution. It was a grave mistake from a number of viewpoints, so clearly a mistake that one of the first things the new government did was to start the amendment process to add a Bill of Rights. How could the Founders have made so grievous and obvious an error?[10]

The words above come from the highly regarded *Decision in Philadelphia* by Christopher and James Lincoln Collier. There are several thoughts or ideas expressed in those words that can be found in every book that I have ever read about the Constitution, and these thoughts or ideas present to me some extremely baffling questions.

The first question involves a lack of knowledge on the part of the public in general. Despite all the books explaining that the Framers[11] did ***not*** write the Bill of Rights and in fact rejected the idea by overwhelming margins, I have never once in my life encountered even one human being who was aware of the fact. Not one. Ever.

And this ignorance extends well beyond the regular Joes of my world. Tune your TV right now to any of the politically oriented channels, and it won't be long before a very highly paid and supposedly knowledgeable person mentions the Founders and their Bill of Rights. This "knowledge" is near universal. The Earth is round, the sun rises in the east, and the Founders/Framers gave us the Bill of Rights.

Maybe you, dear reader, are an exception. But if you are, you should know that you are in rare company. By way of example, we will later read the words of one of the late 20th century's most revered and respected constitutional authorities, a man whose book spent months on *The New York Times* Best Seller list and is probably the best-selling book ever written about the Constitution. And, yes, he thinks the Framers wrote the Bill of Rights.

Of course, there are people in this world who know the truth of the matter. I am sure of this because I've read their books explaining that the Framers had nothing to do with the Bill. But, outside of that extremely narrow slice of humanity writing books on the

U.S. Constitution, (and, as noted above, even those writing books on the Constitution cannot always be counted on to get it right), there appears to be not a soul who is aware of this fact.

And it is a fact. Neither the Framers nor the Founding Fathers had anything to do with the Bill of Rights, except to wisely and overwhelmingly reject the idea. This is a matter of clear and documented historical record. It cannot be denied. History's most revered body of political thinkers had zero interest in one of the most famous political documents of all time, a document that almost all Americans mistakenly believe was their greatest achievement.

One might think that the Framers' lack of interest in a bill of rights would be glaringly obvious to everybody. After all, most everybody knows that the Bill of Rights makes up the first 10 ***amendments*** to the Constitution; had the Framers produced them, the amendments would not be amendments at all.

And then there are *The Federalist Papers*, undoubtedly the most well-known writings ever produced to explain and justify the creation and workings of any government. How many tens of millions of people have read *The Federalist Papers* and found the words of Alexander Hamilton explaining in very simple and direct language the exact and specific reasons for rejecting the idea of a bill of rights? And still the ignorance persists.

And this brings us to a second question, this one involving a lack of knowledge and understanding on the part of those people who write books on the Constitution. As noted above, the Framers are clear not only on the fact that they were not interested in the Bill of Rights, but on ***why*** they thought the Bill was a bad idea.

And yet, in all those books I've read on the Constitution, no author ever seems to understand the reasons for the Framers' rejection of the Bill (ridiculously, simple fatigue at the end of the Constitutional Convention is the most oft-cited reason), and certainly ***none*** of these authors defend the Framers' rejection of the Bill. Ever.

In fact, the first of these issues (lack of understanding) leads to the second. Invariably, we read of the Bill-of-Rights-killing fatigue, followed by a line about how the Framers believed the structure of the Constitution protected individual liberties without a bill of rights. What exactly that "structure" argument means remains largely unexplored and entirely undefended.

When you read that the Framers thought the structure of the Constitution to be the most important guardian of our freedoms, it sounds almost as if they had actually convened for some reason other than protecting our liberties, and that writing the Constitution was something different from and separate from that duty, and that when asked about securing freedoms, the Framers had been caught off guard and quickly mumbled some unconvincing words about "structure." It's like asking a bunch of carpenters after they've finished building a house, "I see you've built this fine house—now tell me, what have you done about providing shelter for its owner?"

Yet a third question, and one to me infinitely more baffling, lies in the quoted accusation above that the Framers did not put ***a*** bill of rights in the Constitution.

We need to be very clear about this: the Framers did not put ***the*** Bill of Rights in the Constitution because there was already ***a*** bill of rights written into the Constitution.

As you will see below, the Framers explain in *The Federalist Papers* and in other writings that there is a bill of rights in the original, unamended Constitution, and they tell us exactly where in the Constitution these protections are found. Yet somehow people write whole books on the subject and manage to entirely miss these vitally important words and ideas, arguably the most important words and ideas ever expressed by that breathtakingly talented assembly of men.

It is one thing to read the Framers' strategy for protecting liberties and believe it inferior to the strategy inherent in the Bill of Rights. It is another thing entirely to falsely accuse the Framers of having no bill of rights in their Constitution at all.

Read the words below.

> I go further, and affirm, that bills of rights, in the sense and to the extent they are contended for, are not only unnecessary in the proposed constitution, but would even be dangerous....
>
> There remains but one other view of this matter to conclude the point. The truth is, after all the declamation we have heard, that the constitution is itself, in every rational sense, and to every useful purpose, A BILL OF RIGHTS.[12]

These are not the words of some Congressional backbencher, writing in his diary or in an obscure publication. These are the words of one of history's most famous men, writing in one of the world's most-read documents: Alexander Hamilton in *Federalist* 84.

His words require explaining. His words require justifying. His words need to be backed up. And, of course, those words ***were*** explained, justified, and backed up—in Madison's records of the Convention, in *The Federalist Papers*, and exhaustively in the state ratifying conventions. And yet the world somehow believes that the Framers placed the Bill of Rights in the Constitution, or, equally erroneously, that there was no bill of rights in the unamended Constitution.

Setting aside the words of the Framers for a moment, one must wonder how anybody could believe that there is no bill of rights in the unamended Constitution. The Framers toiled through that long, oppressive summer, composing a masterwork of historic proportions, and somehow utterly failed to even ***attempt to address*** the question of individual liberty? To believe that, one must not only believe that these liberties were not a central concern of the Framers, but that they were of ***no concern to them at all.*** One must believe that the Framers actually created a totalitarian government. After all, what is the definition of a totalitarian government but one that is empowered for everything and restrained from nothing? Is not a government that has no protections for individual liberty and may do what it wants when it wants a totalitarian one? One must further believe that this totalitarian scheme was ratified by the people in every state in the nation. Who could believe that?

This chapter seeks to remedy all this. Using the simple and straightforward words of the Framers themselves, we will see:

#1: That neither the Framers nor the Founding Fathers had anything to do with the Bill of Rights.

> The numbers don't lie, and the tale is fascinating. Why, for example, did the Bill's most determined opponent end up demanding and then writing the Bill, and why did those who first clamored for it end up rejecting it utterly after it was written?

#2: Exactly ***why*** the Framers rejected the Bill of Rights.

> The Framers rejected the Bill because they correctly predicted that it would destroy freedom and rob us of our liberties. If you're anything like me, the first time you see those words you are shocked with disbelief, filled with skepticism, or perhaps overcome by guffaws at my stupidity and ignorance. How could it possibly be that writing the words "You have the right to x, and y, and z" threatens liberties? Believe me, until the Framers explained it to me, I was every bit as distrustful as you, but it's true.
>
> We will use the words of the Framers themselves to show this, and will not rely in any way on imaginative interpretations, ivory-tower intellectualizing, or the type of Byzantine theorizing favored by lawyers with losing cases. The Framers' reasoning in rejecting the Bill was unimaginably simple, instantly grasped by your average

third grader. It might be believed that tearing down one of the world's most cherished intellectual artifacts would require sophisticated analysis and deep thinking on an Aristotelian level, but this is just not so.

#3: Precisely how the Framers safeguarded all the liberties contained in the Bill of Rights—and uncountable other rights—without ever even mentioning those rights.

The simplicity and, more importantly, the efficacy of their plan is really quite astonishing. Of course, that efficacy depended on the Bill of Rights never being written.

#4: Beyond a doubt that the Framers' strategy for protecting our liberties was infinitely better than the strategy inherent in the rejected Bill of Rights.

This is simply undeniable, and quite apparent when you count the rights we used to have before the Bill of Rights, versus the rights we have now.

#5: That the Bill of Rights is a trick, a scam.

It was written for no reason other than to fool people. ***The Bill changed virtually nothing***, and that was precisely the intent of the man who wrote the Bill. As one author noted, the amendments were "carefully crafted to change not one word of the original Constitution."[13] The Bill's author had no desire to change the Constitution, and the Bill was created to fool those who desired a bill of rights into thinking that he had produced one.

#6: That the Bill of Rights destroyed the U.S. Constitution.

> This is absolutely true. It is not even a tiny hint of an exaggeration. It is not a sentence written to shock in order to sell books. And while it is more accurate to say that the way the Bill of Rights is ***misunderstood*** is what actually destroyed the Constitution, the fact remains—in the absence of the awful bill, we'd still have a Constitution. It was an accident, to be sure. It was not meant to happen. But the Framers predicted it, warned against it, and we should have listened to them.
>
> Of course, the Constitution is not completely destroyed—the federal government can still define and punish piracy, for example—but the most important part of the Constitution, the part that protected our rights, has indeed been obliterated.

The Bill of Rights was not merely a bad idea, a bad change, like, say, Prohibition. No, it went far beyond that, for it introduced a strategy for protecting liberties that was entirely different from the strategy designed by the Framers. But not only was it different, it completely undid the Framers' strategy, obliterating it entirely. As we shall see, these two visions (the Bill of Rights as protector of liberties versus the unamended Constitution as protector of liberties) are mutually exclusive. They represent, with mathematical precision, exact and precise diametric opposites. One is the antithesis of the other. The system of protections the Framers gave us is not diminished by the Bill of Rights; it is not marginalized—it is utterly and absolutely destroyed. The two visions simply cannot exist side by side. Placed in proximity to one another one must die, and indeed, one did.

The damage does not stop there, however. Later, when we examine federalism and federal powers, we will see that not only did the Bill mark the end of the Framers' strategy for protecting our rights, it also entirely obliterated the very foundation of the relationship between the federal and state governments; it morphed the federal government into an organ scarcely different in any way from the state governments. That is a very bad and extremely dangerous thing.

Rejecting the Bill of Rights

When a proposal for a bill of rights was made at the Constitutional Convention in September 1787, the Framers had their chance to burden us with the Bill, but ***only three men*** of 55 favored the motion, the state delegations rejected the proposal unanimously, and the idea was quickly killed.

Still, some maintain that it was the Framers who gave us a bill of rights because the amendments came about in the First Congress, which was, of course, populated by men who were at the Convention and other men who were not at the Convention but are normally referred to as the "Founders."

But this idea will not stand scrutiny either, for it was James Madison, almost single-handedly and with virtually no aid from his fellow Framers or Founders, who ensured that we have a bill of rights. An excellent history of the Bill tells us that what was included and excluded from the Bill were "determined almost entirely by Madison's legislative leadership." Also, the amendments were debated "only because of Madison's stubborn persistence."

Lastly, both Federalists and Anti-Federalists in the House were almost "unanimously opposed" to the amendments, and told Madison of their feelings "in terms that were caustic, scornful, and even derisive."[14] By no stretch of the imagination was the Bill a product of the Framers or the Founders.

And what of Madison himself? It turns out that, despite the foregoing, even he cannot be blamed for the awful Bill, for he was one of the Bill's earliest and most forceful opponents. Politics, however, changed his mind. His unpopular opposition to a bill of rights had contributed to his failed campaign to become one of Virginia's senators in the new government and had subsequently threatened to derail yet another of his campaigns, the one that saw him finally land in the House of Representatives. No, as any decent constitutional text or authority will tell you, the existence of the Bill of Rights is due almost solely to the Anti-Federalists in Virginia who exerted such crushing pressure on Madison.

Still others will say that both Jefferson and Adams were in favor of the Bill. This is true, but irrelevant for several reasons. First, neither of the duo was at the Convention, nor was either of them in the First Congress that produced the Bill. Also, I do not contend that no Framer or Founder was ever in favor of the Bill. The myth that I am demolishing here is the one that goes "The Framers gave us the Bill of Rights," and there is no way on Earth to turn Adams and Jefferson into "the Framers" or even into "the Founding Fathers." By way of illustration, even though Adams and Jefferson died on the same day, you will never see in print the words "The Founding Fathers died, amazingly, on the exact same day, July 4, 1826, precisely 50 years to the day from the signing of the Declaration of Independence."

Additionally, only two of the seven men usually referred to as Founding Fathers were part of the Congress/administration that produced the Bill of Rights. And of the four Founding Fathers at the Convention, ***none*** spoke in favor of the Bill, and the Framer most responsible for the Constitution, Madison, was its most forceful opponent.

Lastly, a mere 21 Framers (38% of that group) were a part of the First Congress, where they made up only 23% of that body, a body in which, again, ***they showed no interest in a bill of rights.***

The "Unnecessary" Bill of Rights versus the Original Bill of Rights

So just what were the Framers' reasons for this wholesale rejection of a bill of rights? As Hamilton noted in *Federalist* 84, there were two reasons: the Bill was both unnecessary and dangerous.

The Bill was unnecessary because, as Hamilton said, the entire Constitution itself was a bill of rights—***protecting rights was the purpose of its creation in the first place.*** This leaves one to wonder how people who write books on the Constitution could possibly overlook that fact.

But where, precisely, are these protections found? What exactly is this strategy for protecting liberty that is the opposite of the one found in the Bill of Rights?

The Framers' strategy for safeguarding liberty against government encroachment was really quite simple—just as simple, in fact (though infinitely more effective) as the strategy behind the Bill of Rights.

They wrote a list. The Framers listed, specified, and detailed the few and defined rights/powers of the federal government. All the uncountable, innumerable scores of rights and powers not found on this small list were off-limits to the federal government and were retained by the people. This list is known as "the Enumeration," and it is found in article I, section 8 of the Constitution—and no, this list contains no provision for the federal government to censor the press or infringe on any of the rights contained in the Bill of Rights. The Enumeration gives the federal government the right to declare war, establish a post office and post roads, raise armies and navies, establish courts, and exercise a few other mundane and necessary powers.

At this point, the Framers directed critics who bemoaned the absence of a bill of rights to the Enumeration and noted with unassailable logic that because the Enumeration contained no provision for the federal government to legislate against cherished liberties, those rights were already protected. A bill of rights was unnecessary because the rights so beloved in what would become our Bill of Rights were already secure, already completely off-limits to federal authority. Why does this breathtakingly simple logic elude so many?

Nowhere in the Enumeration do the people cede to the government the power to regulate the press. Thus, the federal government has no authority whatsoever to do so, or to suppress free speech, or to establish a church, or to seize firearms. The logic and simplicity of their reasoning are undeniable.

The Tiny and "Dangerous" Bill of Very Few and Incomplete Rights

So, why was the Bill of Rights also "dangerous"?[15]

How's this for quick and simple: By listing ***certain*** rights, one creates the impression that those are ***all*** the rights.

Some may instantly grasp the profound and Constitution-destroying difference between the two strategies, but I suspect a good many other readers will scoff, or their shoulders will slump with disappointment at this great and destructive "difference."

"That's it?" they'll ask. "These two lists are so different that the U.S. Constitution was undone by one of them?" To many, these "different" strategies will seem to be not at all different. Interpreting the two lists as being somehow similar would be a huge mistake. The difference is simply absolute in the fullest sense of the word.

We need only consider the following.

The Bill of Rights ***includes*** only a very few rights, excluding all others.

The Enumeration ***excludes*** only a very few rights, protecting all others.

The Framers knew that the people had untold thousands of rights, rights uncountable, rights innumerable. Trying to write down even a fraction of them, as with the Bill of Rights, would be futile, doomed to fail.

> *Enumerate all the rights of men! I am sure, sir, that no gentleman in the late convention would have attempted such a thing.*
>
> — James Wilson, speaking of the Constitutional Convention[16]

That's why the Enumeration was a far better idea. Instead of writing a small list of the rights of the people, the only small list they would create, the Enumeration, would be the one listing the rights/powers of the government.

When Americans think of their rights, when they seek to find what it is that the federal government cannot impose on them, they look to the Bill of Rights, never the Enumeration. This, surely, is an undeniable fact of American life, an ironclad truth that none would ever deny. Refer to any textbook or history book, ask any citizen where in his life government or legislative majorities may not tread, and you will invariably be referred to the Bill of Rights, never the Enumeration. So what is wrong with that, you ask?

Well, before the Bill of Rights, the federal government's power was confined to the Enumeration, while the people had liberties virtually innumerable. Now we have approximately 24, which is fewer than the powers given the federal government in the Enumeration, which stands at 29. How's that for a bargain? The world the Framers gave us (***government's*** powers limited to a small list) is perfectly opposite the world given by the Bill of Rights (***our*** rights limited to a small list).

Because of those ever-evolving and emanating penumbras that are sometimes mysteriously revealed only to very special Supreme Court justices, it is difficult to more precisely number or know our rights. But we do know that before the Bill of Rights, the federal government could not regulate speech, promote a religion, or shackle the press. After the Bill of Rights, it still can't do those things (no improvement here), but it may do ***anything else it wants***.

Our government is, because of the Bill of Rights, virtually all-powerful and operates very nearly without limits or constraints. Suffice it to say that at this point, Americans believe today that our government is absolutely entitled to do virtually anything that is not specifically prohibited by the Bill of Rights. This, of course, stands the Constitution wholly and completely on its head. The exact and precise opposite is true—the government was intended to do nothing that was not specifically "enumerated," to have no powers beyond those laid down in the Enumeration.

If you're a Bill of Rights guy (I more accurately like to call it "the Bill of Very Few Rights"), then you have free speech, freedom of worship, the right to petition the government, and a few others.

If, on the other hand, the Enumeration is more to your liking, then you have all those rights listed above, but you also have tens of thousands (millions?) of other rights, such as the right to marry and to have children, the right to own a home, the right to wear eye shadow, the right to choose a profession, or the right to choose to attend college or to not attend college.

You also had the right, when purchasing chickens, to actually select the specific chickens that you wished to purchase. For a time, though, the federal government believed otherwise. Yes, at one point, the federal government actually made this a criminal offense, and not in some bizarre spasmodic fit of legislative madness in the long-ago 18th century, but in the 20th century. And the government appealed its right to criminalize your deviant, chicken-choosin' psychosis all the way to the Supreme Court.[17] If you're wondering how the federal government could ever do such a thing, well, merely refer to the Bill of Rights, and you will note that, yes, amazingly, the authors did indeed somehow forget to include the "preferred chicken" amendment in that document.

In the next chapter, we will move beyond the Bill of Rights' minor poultry-pickin' problems, beyond dealing with rights in the general sense, and focus on an infinitely more serious problem. ***We will see how the Bill of Rights obliterated protection for what the Framers believed was the most important right of all.***

For most people, largely because of the Bill of Rights, this most important of all rights ***is not even viewed as a right.*** Merely mentioning it as a right feels strange and alien on the tongue. In fact, we have been so thoroughly trained that most people look down upon this most vital of rights as something grubby, a thing that, if cared about too much, marks us as unenlightened or even low class.

We will see how this right is sacrificed on a simply unimaginable scale each and every day by the federal government in virtually every single action that the Leviathan takes. We will see that, indeed, the vast majority of what the federal government does today is prohibited by the Enumeration, but not, sadly, by the Bill of Rights.

For now, however, we need only realize that the Enumeration is nothing more than a far larger, far more comprehensive, far more encompassing bill of rights than its more famous cousin. The Bill of Rights says the federal government will not do 24 things. The Enumeration puts that number easily into the tens of thousands. Under the Enumeration, we had a limited federal government with maximum freedom for the people. With the birth of the Bill of Rights, all that changed. The Enumeration was the soul and the beating heart of the U.S. Constitution; destroy the Enumeration, and you destroy the Constitution.

So, how has the Enumeration, the better and original bill of rights, come to this sad end, unknown and forgotten? How has this extraordinary and amazing thing come to pass? Again, it is the Bill of Rights itself that is almost entirely responsible for this turn of events. Such an occurrence was, of course, brilliantly predicted by the Framers and others at the time, and they put their thoughts on paper for all the world to see.

> *In a government consisting of enumerated powers, such as is proposed for the United States, a bill of rights would not only be unnecessary, but, in my humble judgment, highly*

imprudent. In all societies, there are many powers and rights, which cannot be particularly enumerated. A bill of rights annexed to a constitution, is an enumeration of the powers reserved. If we attempt an enumeration, every thing that is not enumerated, is presumed to be given. The consequence is, that an imperfect enumeration would throw all implied power into the scale of the government; and the rights of the people would be rendered incomplete. On the other hand, an implied enumeration of the powers of government, reserves all implied power to the people; and, by that means the constitution becomes incomplete; but of the two it is much safer to run the risk on the side of the constitution; for an omission in the enumeration of the powers of government, is neither so dangerous, nor important, as an omission in the enumeration of the rights of the people.

— James Wilson[18]

A proposition to adopt a measure that would have supposed that we were throwing into the general government every power not expressly reserved by the people, would have been spurned at, in that house (the Convention), with the greatest indignation....In a government possessed of enumerated powers, such a measure would be not only unnecessary, but preposterous and dangerous.

— James Wilson[19]

It has been objected also against a bill of rights, that, by enumerating particular exceptions to the grant of power, it would disparage those rights which were not placed in the enumeration; and it might follow, by implication, that those rights that were not placed in that enumeration, that those rights which were not singled out, were intended to be assigned into the hands of the General Government, and were consequently insecure.

— James Madison[20]

I go further, and affirm, that bills of rights, in the sense and to the extent they are contended for, are not only unnecessary in the proposed constitution, but would even be dangerous. They would contain various exceptions to powers not granted; and on this very account, would afford a colourable pretext to claim more than were granted. For why declare that things shall not be done, which there is no power to do? Why, for instance, should it be said, that the liberty of the press shall not be restrained, when no power is given by which restrictions may be imposed?

— Alexander Hamilton[21]

*My own opinion has always been in favour of a bill of rights;[22] provided it be so framed as not to imply powers not meant to be included in the **enumeration** [emphasis added]. At the same time, I have never thought the omission*

> *a material defect, nor been anxious to supply it even by subsequent [emphasis in original] amendment, for any other reason than that it is anxiously desired by others. I have favoured it because I supposed it might be of use, and, if properly executed, could not be of disservice. I have not viewed it [the Bill of Rights] in an important light.*
>
> *1. Because I conceive that in a certain degree... the rights in question are reserved by the manner in which the federal powers are granted....*
>
> *3. Because the* ***limited powers of the federal Government*** *[emphasis added], and the jealousy of the subordinate governments, afford a security which has not existed in the case of the state governments, and exists in no other.*
>
> — James Madison[23]

The following two quotations come from Justice Thomas McKean, delegate to the Pennsylvania ratifying convention.

> The whole plan of government [of the Constitution] is nothing more than a bill of rights.[24]
>
> It has already been incontrovertibly shown that on the present occasion a bill of rights was totally unnecessary, and that it might be accompanied with some inconveniency and danger, if there was any defect in the attempt to enumerate the privileges of the people.[25]

McKean also asks (rhetorically and brilliantly), if a person wants to sell 250 of his 1,000 acres, is it necessary to "reserve" the other 750?[26] In other words, when you show up at my house to buy my car, do I have to attach to the bill of sale a document listing all the many thousands of my other possessions that I am ***not*** selling to you?

This fear, that listing certain rights would tend to "disparage" other rights not listed,[27] was plainly obvious and logical enough to compel that the last two amendments of the Bill of Rights would hammer home the point. Sadly, these last two amendments are just like the Enumeration itself: entirely unknown, unremembered, unenforced, and unloved. Have you ***ever*** in your life heard somebody, anybody, invoke the Ninth or Tenth Amendment as a restraint on federal power? The Ninth and Tenth Amendments are simply and entirely worthless.

> Article IX. The enumeration in the Constitution, of certain rights, shall not be construed to deny or disparage others retained by the people.[28]

In other words, just because we list a very few rights for the people in this here Bill of Rights, don't think that those are all they have. There are more. How many more? Well, read the next amendment.

> Article X. The powers not delegated to the United States by the Constitution, nor prohibited by it to the States, are reserved to the States respectively, or to the people.[29]

In other words, all the awesome and numberless powers not given to the federal government in the Constitution and not denied to the states (***much*** more on powers denied to the states later) by the same Constitution remain with the states, the people, or both.

You might notice something else very important in those last two amendments. Not only are they saying that you have more rights than those listed in the Bill of Very Few Rights, but they make plain the fact, as noted earlier, that the Bill of Rights changed nothing, accomplished nothing. Again, that was the intent.

The Ninth and Tenth Amendments say nothing on their own; they cannot stand in isolation. They specify no rights or powers. They merely refer back to the unamended Constitution itself and say, "You want to know your rights? Look here."

So, what is behind the fact that the Bill of Rights did not really amend, and was not intended to amend, the Constitution? Why write it, then? It helps to realize that James Madison is known as "The Father of the Constitution." He is also known as "The Father of the Bill of Rights." There's a clue in that.

Madison was, understandably, a partisan of the constitution that he had written. The Anti-Federalists were not. They were vehemently opposed to the new federal government created by that document and were pushing for a bill of rights to radically alter it, or even for a second convention to create a new government entirely from scratch. Madison did not want to change the constitution that he had written, so he wrote a bill of rights that indeed did not change in any meaningful way "his" constitution. Simple.

Madison's amendments were not designed to fool Anti-Federalist leadership, men like Patrick Henry, who, in fact, rejected the Bill of Rights, precisely because it changed nothing. The amendments were, however, meant to fool the masses, the people. And to the extent that the people really did want the Bill (there is debate as to how motivated the people really were for amendments versus how much the push had to do with powerful, elite leadership by the likes of men like Henry), Madison succeeded.

The great sad irony here is that the Anti-Federalists' push for a bill of rights eventually turned the federal government into the all-powerful monster that they feared.

Those skeptical of the Enumeration might point out that because it does not specify rights, it is ever so slightly more complex and abstract than the Bill of Rights, and given widespread voter apathy or ignorance, the Bill of Very Few Rights is still better than the Enumeration. If there were only the Enumeration, the thinking goes, stupendously ignorant Americans would today have no knowledge of the Enumeration whatsoever. In other words, 24 rights are better than none.

I find this idea simply ridiculous. We know that with or without a bill of rights, the subject of our liberties time and time and time again over the last 200+ years has been the catalyst of heated and intense controversy, litigation, legislation, and even armed conflict. With or without a bill of rights, the questions of just what our constitutional rights are, where in that document they are found, and how they are protected would, therefore, be extremely familiar to all Americans—***every bit as familiar as the Bill of Rights***.

If, from day one, and stretching 200+ years into the future, you had never once found your rights other than in the Enumeration, then you'd be very unlikely ever to forget the Enumeration. Is the Bill of Rights in any danger of being forgotten? If Congress were tomorrow to propose to abolish several newspapers because Congress found them offensive, how likely is it that the people would somehow forget the Bill of Rights and think the proposal legal and constitutional?

Without a bill of rights, however, Americans long, long ago, would have been forced to know something of the context of the creation and ratification of the Constitution, and something of the thoughts of the men who wrote it.

Therefore, without a bill of rights, but with better than 200 years of history behind us, every schoolchild would be able to recite with complete confidence a vague yet true statement to the effect that "We have lots of rights. The federal government's rights are few and defined, and they are chiefly found in our Constitution in Article I, Section VIII. A new federal government proposal to regulate the press because of, say, a recent spate of "fake news" is not one of the powers granted the federal government. The proposal is, therefore, illegal."

Instead of memorizing simply "freedom of speech, religion, and press" and nothing else, we would have memorized a few words to sum up James Madison below in *Federalist* 45.

> The powers delegated by the proposed constitution to the federal government, are few and defined. Those which

> are to remain in the state governments, are numerous and indefinite. The former will be exercised principally on external objects, as war, peace, negotiation, and foreign commerce; with which last the power of taxation will, for the most part, be connected. The powers reserved to the several states will extend to all the objects, which, in the ordinary course of affairs, concern the lives, liberties, and properties of the people; and the internal order, improvement, and prosperity of the state.
>
> The operations of the federal government will be most extensive and important in times of war and danger; those of the state governments in times of peace and security.[30]

The Bill of Very Few Rights is so inseparably linked with the Framers, the Founders, or both in our minds that it is simply impossible for us to see that it is ***contradictory*** in nature to the Constitution and that it really does stand the Constitution on its head, destroying it in the process.

The source of this confusion lies very simply in the fact that people believe both documents were written by the same men at the same time. If that were true, clearly there should be no contradiction. Therefore, the mind balks at the contradiction, producing confusion. This would not happen if people knew the documents were produced by different men, with different agendas, at different times.

If Joe writes a document and three years later Susie writes a document, we would easily grasp and understand if they were contradictory. We would not ***expect*** uniformity. Our logical minds would not ***demand*** uniformity. But if a group of men writes one document on one occasion, we expect that document to be logically consistent throughout. We will revisit this mind-bending confusion in chapter 9.

One last word about bills of rights in general. In *Federalist* 84 and at the Pennsylvania ratifying convention, we find Hamilton and James Wilson, respectively, remarking brilliantly on those times and places where bills of rights were more logical and served man, rather than stealing his liberties. They had their place in situations where the governed had few if any rights before managing to wrest, usually by force of arms, some meager scraps from their rulers.

When the king is presumed to possess all legislative powers, and the people are able to snatch a few precious liberties from the royal grip, then it makes all the sense in the world to list those few rights. But with our Constitution, the American people were in ***precisely the opposite situation***; all legislative power rested with the people from the start. It made far more sense in our case to list the few treasured liberties that we the people were willing to compromise for the necessity of government.

We stole an idea from serfs, whose situation was exactly opposite ours, ***and we became them***. They listed a few rights (the only ones they had); we then followed their lead and listed a few rights, and they ***became*** the only ones we have. How amazingly ironic!

Right now would be a good time to dispel the myth about the Second Amendment meaning only "state-controlled militias are acceptable," but I'd like to first turn to the most important right of them all. While you've probably never heard of this right because greedy and clever politicians who want all your cash have been ramming the Bill of Very Few Rights down your gullet since about five seconds after you exited the womb, it is indeed a right as sacred and unalienable as your speech rights.

However, if you'd rather read about guns first, please feel free to turn to chapter 4 now.

CHAPTER TWO

Property Rights and Your Sacred Paycheck

"THE LAWS OF GOD"[31]

The only word that fits when describing the Framers' attitude toward protecting your property is "obsession." Therefore, the first thing we must do, right now, is define exactly what the Framers meant by the word "property." It absolutely and positively does ***not*** merely mean land, as many believe.

Let us check with James Madison in a vitally important quotation that we will examine in full a bit later.

> A man's land, or merchandise, or money, is called his property.[32]

Money is property…If you want some modern confirmations of that formulation, a Google search will reveal the truth of this in seconds. Mine turned up Paul Larkin writing for the Heritage Foundation.

> Accordingly, the Founders' generation understood that property included the right to possess, use, enjoy, and dispose of land, commodities, currency, or their equivalents.[33]

Also, the American Policy Center recently ran an article correcting the mistaken notion that property refers to landed estates. The author also states that in 1700s America, property was better understood. He writes, "Property, and the ability to own and control it, was ***life itself***."[34]

So, no; neither the Framers nor the philosophy behind property rights itself discriminate in their views on what property means. The landed estate of the great man in the great house is no more sacred, no more deserving of government protection than are his shoelaces or his coffee cups, and certainly no more sacred than the coins the poor laborer receives for plowing the great man's fields.

It really must be this way, of course. After all, can you think of a more morally bankrupt philosophy than one that would proclaim that if you are wealthy enough or lucky enough to own land, then you are entitled to some government protection that a mere laborer is not entitled to?

Now that we know the definition of property (your paycheck), let us see what value the Framers placed on it. You might want to read the last quotation twice just to let it sink in.

---

*The moment the idea is admitted into society, that property is not as sacred as the laws of God, and that there is not a force of law and public justice to protect it, anarchy and tyranny commence. If "*THOU SHALT NOT COVET,*" and "*THOU SHALT NOT STEAL,*" were not commandments of Heaven, they must be made inviolable precepts in every society before it can be civilized or made free.*

— JOHN ADAMS[35]

Property is surely a right of mankind as really as liberty.

— JOHN ADAMS[36]

Property must be secured, or liberty cannot exist.

— JOHN ADAMS[37]

Government is instituted to protect property of every sort; as well that which lies in the various rights of individuals, as that which the term particularly expresses. This being the end of government, that alone is a just government, which impartially secures to every man, whatever is his own.

— JAMES MADISON[38]

The primary objects of civil society are the security of property and public safety.

— James Madison[39]

Lastly, Forrest McDonald tells us that the Framers believed that the object of government was the protection of life, liberty, and property. All but four of the Framers, that is—but three of those four disagreed with that formulation because they actually "put the protection of property ***ahead*** of liberty as the main object of society."[40]

I still vividly remember the exact moment I found out that my paycheck was a sacred right. I was sitting in a classroom in Texas, and a professor changed my life. We were reading from the book *The People Shall Judge*. The book quotes the Framers/Founders extensively. Their obsession with and endless use of the word "property" was quite surprising to me.

I was thinking to myself, "Boy! These guys were ***really*** concerned about their land!" And I was a little disappointed.

I also thought the material was out of date. I kept thinking, "Yeah, I know. Way back when, people saw their land as some sacred thing that was passed down through the generations, and their land defined them, and linked them to their ancestors and their hallowed this-and-that, blah, blah, blah." Snatches of Scarlett O'Hara's father's speech on the subject were dancing around in my head. Again, this all seemed a bit dated. Nobody thought that way in the 1990s; we were all far more concerned about our certificates of deposit and the DJIA than we were about land.

Also, I was one of those youth eager to read the usual saccharine, over-the-top rhetoric about the Bill of Rights. I felt a tad let down by this obsession with personal wealth. Sadly for me, we had read almost ***nothing*** on any of the rights found in the Bill of Rights.

And then the professor held up his index finger, and he said, "Remember; ***money*** is property!"

To this very day, well over 30 years later, that moment stands as one of the most important in my life. And I can honestly say that the rightness of the Framers' words was instantly apparent to me. (I'm lucky that way. I find that most people, even staunch conservatives, have been so brainwashed that they resist, passionately, the "property = money = a right" equation.)

In a flash, it was suddenly obvious to my libertarian-leaning mind that, except in narrowly tailored circumstances that we'll cover shortly, not only may no human tell me what I can or cannot say, but no human ever has any claim to even one dime of the money that is mine.

No, this does not mean that taxation is criminal. More on this later, but taxes are absolutely legitimate and entirely necessary. And while my right to my money is just as unalienable as my right to worship and should be treated with at least as much reverence, it is, like ***all*** rights in civil society, necessarily and justifiably compromised. You can't shout fire in a crowded theater, and you must pay taxes.

However, while the government should never oppress my speech rights just because some may find my speech offensive, the government also should never oppress my property rights for breathtakingly nonsensical reasons—like the trash that the DOGE has been uncovering, or a Woodstock concert museum.

When New York senators tried to take my money for a museum dedicated to the cultural glories of the Woodstock concert, it was not merely annoying or stupid, ***it was a crime***. Even ***attempting*** to oppress my property rights for their little museum was every bit as much a crime as if they had attempted to oppress my speech rights by preventing me from protesting their ridiculous and corrupt scheme.

After all, how can it possibly be legitimate for clients in New York to tap the shoulders of their senators and ask those senators to seize ***your*** money and give it to ***them***? Why should your paycheck be the plaything of politicians who live in states thousands of miles from you? Why and how is such a thing even legal? Actually, when the Constitution was understood and respected, this kind of thing was ***not*** legal, and that's why federal spending as a percentage of GDP averaged ***less than 4%*** for the nation's first 130 years.[41] More on that later.

From the moment I'd become even a bit politically aware, I knew all about some of the insanely ridiculous things (again, hat tip to DOGE here) that the federal government spent my money on. You've heard of them; we've ***all*** heard of them. Some of these things are so flat-out bizarre, they might actually be hilarious if they weren't so expensive.

After reading the Framers' words, though, I suddenly realized that these things were not just infuriating in their stupidity, they were irredeemably corrupt—corrupt to their core. These expenditures were blatant theft, immoral and tyrannical at the same time.

We've come now to the point of this chapter. It may be an impossible uphill struggle, but my goal here is to make you feel deep in your bones that the government expenditures you've spent a lifetime laughing at are not merely ridiculous, or even outrageous. They are every bit as immoral and corrupt and wrong as the oppression of free speech.

An uphill struggle indeed...Can you imagine a politician campaigning on a promise to suppress your free speech? And yet, so thoroughly trained are we in surrendering our cash that in every election cycle there are dozens of candidates who openly, brazenly, and proudly swear to the high heavens that they have great plans to seize even more of your money. And they win just as many elections as they lose.

I can think of three things that keep people from recognizing the sacred nature of their earnings—all three powerful in their ability to deceive, but none in any way legitimate.

First, there's our old friend the Bill of Very Few Rights, jumping up and down, yammering about free speech while politicians fight with each other over who gets the biggest share of your cash. Never forget—the Bill of Rights is perhaps the greatest con of all time. It convinced a virtuous, industrious, and free people that their paychecks were the legitimate playthings of every single elected official in the nation and that it was unquestionably legitimate for politicians to seize your property to enrich others and to buy votes. The Bill of Rights has helped to turn us into the most highly trained, profit-producing monkeys in all history.

Second, for all our lives, the supremely bankrupt notion that there is something somehow grubby and tainted about money and mere commerce has been pounded into our skulls with sledgehammers. This despite the incomparable Samuel Johnson instructing us that "There are few ways in which a man can be more innocently employed than in getting money."[42] Also, isn't it strange how politicians are always so eager to get their mitts on our grubby cash in order to give it to somebody else in exchange for votes? Does your property stop being grubby when given to others?

And one more thing. The ***only*** reason that I've not lived a short, ugly life of unendurable toil, hardship, and soul-crushing menial labor is because a lot of people before me (investors, inventors, industrialists, capitalists) have wanted to—and have succeeded in—making a lot of grubby cash. Do people not see? You can make grubby money or you can live in a cave and fight off feral beasts for the privilege of eating bugs. It's that simple.

Last, there ***is*** one very significant difference between our money and our other sacred rights. As noted earlier, in order for government to exist, it ***must*** seize somebody's cash. Taxation is entirely legitimate. There is no other way. The same, however, is not true about most of our other rights. Governments can exist, thrive, and function smoothly even if they have nearly limitless respect for gun rights, free speech, or freedom of worship. Money's different, though. If you want the blessings of government, if you want to rise above the dreaded state of nature where life is—I'm sure you've heard—"nasty, brutish, and short,"[43] then you must have government, and you must pay for it.

In order to exist, government must, frequently and regularly, seize your cash. It's easy to see how this leads to the crazy notion that there's really nothing at all special about your property. When the federal government takes your money and gives it to mohair producers, or multinational firms for their overseas advertising, or farmers in the form of price supports, or any one of hundreds of other special interest groups in whatever inventive fashion, then this is somehow seen as legitimate. Stupid and wasteful at times, certainly, but ***never*** immoral, ***never*** a violation of our sacred, natural rights. It just does not occur to people that their money should be treated precisely like all their sacred rights—infringed on, taken, or seized minimally, and only when necessary.

So many people, when looking at the type of spending mentioned above, will chime in here that government spending like this is just the inevitable and legitimate cost of doing business, the price we pay for living in a civil society that protects our lives and cleans the streets. After all, we can never—and will never—all agree on every government expense.

Nonsense! And the Framers knew better. They thought enough of your paycheck to make sure the kind of federal government spending noted above was unconstitutional (much more on the constitutional versus the unconstitutional in chapter 8). It was not some mistake, oversight, or forgetfulness that kept those kinds of powers from being assigned to the federal government, from being listed in the Enumeration.

Again, this is why the Enumeration is so much better than the Bill of Very Few Rights. It's also the reason politicians ***love*** the Bill of Rights—read those amendments and place your finger on that part that prevents the government from taking ***100% of your property*** and giving it to the Department of Education or even to a foreign nation for "humanitarian aid."

And, until the Supreme Court lost its nerve in the 1930s, that kind of federal spending hardly existed.

As noted earlier, in the 130 years before World War II, federal spending as a percentage of GDP averaged ***less than 4%***.[44] Now it's well over 20%.[45] In 2021, ***it was 35%***.[46]

As you will see when you read all the others that are to come, the quotations that begin this chapter are neither cherry-picked nor aberrations.

The Framers believed more passionately in your right to keep your money than they did in anything mentioned in the First Amendment, and references to money, property, taxes, etc., appear in *The Federalist Papers* ***more than 17 times as often*** as the First Amendment rights ***combined***.

Especially in today's environment, when people consider those sweat-stained dollars in their pockets as the fruits of mere commerce, dirty and grubby in nature, it is simply not possible to overstate the point that the Framers believed that your money was among the most precious of your rights.

The idea that our paychecks are on an equal footing with such things as the right to choose our own lifestyles is unknown to almost all Americans. It is, further, nothing short of incomprehensible to us. Most of us, upon hearing that our paychecks, those ugly little dollar bills of ours, represent rights as sacred and unalienable as our speech rights will react with ridicule, shock, or disdain, for nothing could be so totally alien, so utterly foreign, and so simply outrageous as that claim. This notion is simply beyond the pale.

I believe, however, that just a bit more reflection on the subject can convince most people of the truth of the proposition. The notion that property is and should be as sacred as everything else that makes up freedom and self-determination becomes obvious with some thoughtful consideration.

First, most Americans are already deeply committed to and passionate believers in property rights—they just don't know it. I've said a few times that you've never heard of property rights, but that's not entirely true. You've actually heard of them frequently and for your entire life—but you know property rights by different names. Let's go back to that James Madison quotation with which we began this chapter. This time, we'll quote him in full.

> This term [property], in its particular application, means "that dominion which one man claims and exercises over

> the external things of the world, in exclusion of every other individual."
>
> In its larger and juster meaning, it embraces everything to which a man may attach a value and have a right; and *which leaves to everyone else the like advantage* [emphasis in original].
>
> In the former sense, a man's land, or merchandise, or money, is called his property.
>
> In the latter sense, a man has a property in his opinions and the free communication of them.
>
> He has a property of peculiar value in his religious opinions, and in the profession and practice dictated by them.
>
> He has a property very dear to him in the safety and liberty of his person. He has an equal property in the free use of his faculties, and free choice of the objects on which to employ them. In a word, as a man is said to have a right to his property, he may be equally said to have a property in his rights.[47]

The above is pretty clear. Your free speech rights, and your right to worship as you choose, and your right to self-defense, and your freedom of thought and of opinion and of conscience, ***every single thing, without exception,*** that makes up today's pantheon of precious and sacred rights, is encompassed, and always has been, by the term "property rights." And the truth of that goes back to at least the 17th century and John Locke,[48] the single most significant influence on the Framers and their thoughts on property.

In other words, this country has, for at least the entirety of my life, been in thrall to property rights. It's just that someone has done a wonderful job of deleting the "property" part.

And the fact that they are called property rights and not "conscience rights" is no accident. Property rights may not be any more sacred than our other rights, but, in a political context at least, they are certainly the most important of our rights.

We noted earlier that a philosophy of property rights that includes land but not dollar bills is clearly illegitimate and illogical. So too is a philosophy that says, in the American tradition, "I have a right to do or to say anything that does no harm to others," but somehow excludes from that statement the keeping of one's own money.

A man proclaims that he has every right to act and speak in bizarre, offensive, and revolting ways. He stands in the public square and spits on your nation, heritage, culture, and religion, and he proudly worships Satan or a tree stump.

Almost all Americans would say, "Those are his rights! Nothing that he has said or done harms me or harms others."

Another man stands up and says "I want merely to keep my paycheck in my pocket and out of the hands of Senators Clinton and Schumer and their friends who want my cash for a Woodstock museum. This is my sacred right and harms no others."

How many Americans agree with the second man? Virtually zero. Sure, we understand his desire, but that part about keeping his money being a sacred right? We scoff. Keeping his money is certainly not, and never will be, and cannot ever be, a sacred right.

That is wrong. It is illegitimate and illogical. Who was this god who stood before the world and declared that our sacred rights of conscience did not include keeping our money? You believe in tree stump worship. I believe in keeping my money. How is one a right and not the other? Who gets to decide that I'm being common and grubby, while tree stump guy is nurturing his soul? Who separated conscience from cash, marking cash as an unholy desire? Who said that only the individual can declare his own conscience, and that it can be ***anything*** in heaven or earth that harms no others, ***except*** keeping what he has earned? Where is the logic in that? Who declared that money is off-limits? Not John Locke or the Framers, the most brilliant men ever assembled in one place at one time. No, that idea is a modern invention, one pushed by politicians who do not care about any of your aberrant thoughts or actions just so long as the cash keeps flowing, so long as your money can be seized by them and handed to others in exchange for votes.

So, what is at first alien or ludicrous is really nothing more than post–World War II American liberal thought, instantly recognized and accepted by almost all. What is at first shocking, is, on second evaluation, plainly obvious.

The Natural Liberty of Man is to be free from any Superior Power on Earth, and not to be under the Will or Legislative Authority of Man, but to have only the Law of Nature for his Rule.

— John Locke[49]

The legitimate powers of government extend to such acts only as are injurious to others.

— Thomas Jefferson[50]

This, after all, is the very heart and soul of modern liberal thought. Therefore, those whose speech is as close to pure evil as speech can become, such as the Nazis demonstrating in front of Holocaust survivors in Skokie, Illinois, are every bit as protected by law as those who would write politically motivated letters to their local newspapers. Can it really be that taunting Holocaust survivors is okay, but merely keeping your money is outrageous?

If we are really entitled to engage in activities that do not harm others, why do we so easily accept that this philosophy, which covers our social, political, religious, and moral existence, does ***not*** include our economic activity, which most people engage in more than all others? If we really believe that we are in any significant way free, why are we so willing to exclude the one activity that virtually the whole of humanity spends most of its waking time engaged in—the pursuit of property?

How is it that zealously protecting weird and outlandish behavior, engaged in by various and sundry freaks, is government's sacred charge, to be regulated only under certain very extreme circumstances, but when a ditch is dug, a window is washed, or an automobile is repaired, the government can insert itself into the equation for virtually any reason on Earth, cutting itself in for a limitless supply of the pie to finance bizarre "studies," a bike path, a student loan, or a highway to be named for a congressman and placed in his district three thousand miles from the taxpayers who financed it?

There is just no intellectually good reason why repugnant actions that harm no others should receive constitutional protection while the working actions of a ditchdigger, window washer, or mechanic that harm no others—and indeed are a valuable resource—receive no protection whatsoever.

And again, we do willingly and rightfully compromise our rights, including property rights, when living in civil society. It is an absolute requirement. As noted earlier, there can be no other way. But why, upon entering civil society, do we surrender as little as is humanly possible of our speech and other rights, while simultaneously surrendering ***100% of our property rights***? And, yes, 100% is the correct number, for there is ***no*** limiting principle in today's government that would prohibit a seizure of all my property for virtually any reason imaginable.

Let us forget Locke for a moment. Forget our Constitution, the Framers, and the Founding Fathers, too. For you need not have heard of any of them to be familiar with today's American credo, which goes something like this: "No man or institution may tell me how to live my life. I am free to be my own person, and self-determination is my right."

Or, to quote the famously liberal Supreme Court Justice Harry Blackmun in one of his well-known dissents,

> "The most comprehensive of rights and the right most valued by civilized men" [is] "the right to be let alone"… "[T]he concept of privacy embodies the 'moral fact that a person belongs to himself and not others nor to society as a whole.'"[51]

If you accept this credo, then you must accept that a laborer should not have to surrender his wages to support another human being. For it is a simple and undeniable fact that what freedom is, what was sacred in the Framers' and Locke's worldview was self-determination and all the many things that that means. And when somebody is coerced to reject his true beliefs or maintain silence about his ideas or is made to labor for the benefit of another, then he has lost liberty, lost self-determination. He is not free.

One more philosophical note on your right to your money. File this under the "strange bedfellows" category, but "my body, my right" people (anti-vaxxers, pro-choicers, etc.) should appreciate this.

Locke instructs that it is the labor necessary to acquire property that imbues it with its special nature. When a man works to acquire or create property, the very nature of the property changes—its existence becomes intertwined with the labor of its creator.

The thing created is a part of the creator. Simply put, a man owns his own labor and his own person. Indeed, a man's labor is an extension of his very self. ***When they take your money, they are taking a part of you!***

People realize this easily enough, I believe, when they see a homesteader building a cabin and growing crops. If a man chooses, however, to not take his property in the form of an acre of corn and a bunch of chickens, but instead turns his labor (his very self) into a paycheck after analyzing spreadsheets for 40 hours a week, people lose sight of the principle. That's a mistake—the two situations are logically identical.

> *Though the Earth, and all inferior Creatures be common to all Men, yet every Man has a Property in his own Person. This no Body has any Right to but himself. The Labour of his Body, and the Work of his Hands, we may say, are properly his. Whatsoever then he removes out of the State that Nature hath provided, and left it in, he hath mixed his Labour with, and joyned to it something that is his own, and thereby makes it his Property. It being by him removed from the common State Nature placed it in, it hath by this labour something annexed to it, that excludes the common right of other Men. For this Labour being the unquestionable Property of the Labourer, no Man but he can have a right to what that is once joyned to, at least where there is enough, and as good left in common for others.*
>
> — John Locke[52]

Why Are Property Rights the Most Important of All Rights?

Property rights are more important than free speech? (Gasp!) Yes, and as soon as we all stop entertaining the patently ridiculous, virtue signaling, self-congratulatory little fantasy that goes, "I may disapprove of what you say, but I will defend to the death your right to say it,"[53] then the world will be a much better place.

To see why property rights are the most important, we will first consult James Madison writing in *Federalist* 10, widely regarded as the best and most famous of those essays. What does Madison have to say about property in this brilliant piece?

Madison begins by saying that one of the best aspects of the proposed Union is "its tendency to break and control the violence of faction."[54] A "faction" is what today we call a special interest group.

He refers to the "instability, injustice, and confusion" that factions bring about.[55] Many things give rise to society's factions, Madison notes, "But the most common and durable source of factions, has been ***the various and unequal distribution of property***."[56]

Property is unequally distributed because of "The diversity in the faculties of men."[57]

And, more importantly, "The protection of these faculties, is the ***first*** object of government."[58]

Can it get simpler than this? The chief cause of civil strife is the fact that men cannot stop coveting the property of other men, and the "***first*** object" of government is to protect said property.

Madison goes on to say that "justice" ought to decide legislative questions, not the will of the majority acting through a legislature, for this sets up the majority as judges in their own cause.[59] And what are the legislative topics that most concern Madison? No cookie for guessing something other than free speech or a free press. Nor is he most concerned with the right to protest or worship or own guns. No, the most pressing questions involve creditors versus debtors, tariffs as they relate to domestic manufacturers versus foreign manufacturers, and the landed class versus the manufacturing class.[60] So…money, money, and money again. And let's not forget questions of taxation in which,

> Every shilling with which they [the majority] over-burden the inferior number, is a shilling saved to their own pockets.[61]

Money again. Madison closes by noting that a large and extended republic, such as proposed for the nation, provides the remedy to control factions. This is because factions would have a difficult time spreading their mischief and coordinating their efforts over distances and populations large enough to affect the national legislature.[62]

What poison, exactly, is it that these factions will be unable to spread through the nation? Hint—it's not their desire to crush free speech. ***Yet again***, we see that his concern is for money and property.

> A rage for paper money, for an abolition of debts, for an equal division of property, or for any other improper or wicked project, will be less apt to pervade the whole body of the union, than a particular member of it.[63]

In summation, property is the foremost catalyst of the conflicts (both political and armed) that make government necessary in the first place, and government's role is not to redistribute this property, but to secure it with its rightful possessor.

When speaking of the importance of property, we might also note here that the immediate and most important causes of our revolution were the Stamp Act, the Townshend Acts, the Sugar Act, and the Tea Act. In other words, money, money, money, and money again.

Also, more importantly, we will see in the next chapter that it was repeated assaults on property—in this case pure cash (paper money and gold/silver coin)—that led not only to the Revolution, but to the creation of the Constitution itself.

Let us be clear—the most immediate and pressing cause for the calling of the Constitutional Convention and the creation of the U.S. Constitution ***was to stop one group of Americans from continuing to steal money from another group of Americans.*** The Convention was called to protect money—not free speech, or freedom of religion, or the right to keep and bear arms. It was called to protect ***money***.

And all this obsession with property should come as no surprise. It is a plain and simple fact that property/money ***is*** at the center of ***your*** universe, and this has nothing to do with governments, philosophers, political thinkers, or anything else outside of and separate from you. If you're anything approaching normal, you've spent your entire life pursuing property, and no matter how much you have, you want more. And you will probably carry that desire for more literally until the day you die. For better or worse, that's just how almost all of us operate. Lots of people claim to have no interest in the Powerball; maybe one in 1,000 of them means it.

Property/money is also the lifeblood of politics and government, and any government charter that does not take these facts into account will almost certainly not protect the property of anybody but the ruling class.

And while Americans now have vastly more property than did our forefathers, that in no way changes the sanctity of its nature, as some would argue. Truly, nothing has changed where property is concerned. Even today, even here in the United States, a nation awash in prosperity, we spend roughly half our waking lives, for 50 years or more, in the pursuit of property. Yes, even today, property still equals health, peace, security, and, sometimes, happiness.

When the day comes that property is so plentiful that our government ceases taking it from us to give to others, one might then argue that things have changed, but until then, property remains what it has always been: a vital, sacred right.

It may seem grubby, it may seem common, it is not the stuff of epic poems and majestic rhetoric, but property keeps us alive, and for the few of us fortunate enough to live under governments that allow even a moderately unrestricted pursuit of it, property has raised us from shortened lives of ugly, backbreaking toil and made us healthy, wealthy, secure, and comfortable. How many greater gifts are to be found on this Earth?

These are the reasons property rights are so vital, and these are the reasons the Framers wrote so much about them.

In *The Federalist Papers*, for example, forms of the four words below, dealing with only one unalienable right, appear 316 times.

- Money: 47
- Tax: 133
- Revenue: 75
- Property: 61

This is more than ***17 times*** as often as the words below, which deal with your "big three" First Amendment rights.

- Religion: 7
- Speech : 0
- Press: 8
- Newspaper: 3

"Money" appears more than twice as often as all the words in the second set combined.

"Tax" appears more than seven times as often as all the words in the second set combined.

"Revenue" appears more than four times as often as all the words in the second set combined.

"Property" appears more than three times as often as all the words in the second set combined.

Similar numbers occur within the Constitution itself, even after the Bill of Rights is included. The four "money" words appear more than four times as often as the words in the second group. Indeed, ***none***[64] of the words from the second group appears in the original, unamended Constitution.

In the next chapter, we will see how assaults on property rights led to the creation of the Constitution.

> *The personal right to acquire property, which is a natural right, gives to property, when acquired, a right to protection, as a social right.*
>
> — James Madison[65]

> *One great [object] of [Government] is personal protection and the security of Property.*
>
> — Alexander Hamilton[66]

Government has no other end but the preservation of Property.

— John Locke[67]

The absolute rights of Englishmen...are the rights of personal security, personal liberty, and of private property.

— James Otis[68]

Men cannot be happy, without Freedom; nor free, without Security of Property; nor so secure, unless the sole Power to dispose of it be lodged in themselves.

— John Dickinson[69]

That all men are by nature equally free and independent and have certain inherent rights, of which, when they enter into a state of society, they cannot, by any compact, deprive or divest their posterity; namely, the enjoyment of life and liberty, with the means of acquiring and possessing property, and pursuing and obtaining happiness and safety.

— George Mason[70]

But who would trust his life, liberty, and property to a madman, or an assembly of them? It would be safer to confide in knaves. Five hundred or five thousand together, in an assembly, are not less liable to this extravagance than one.

— John Adams[71]

CHAPTER THREE

The Welfare Program That Birthed a Nation

"MARK OF THE BEAST"[72]

Why do we have a constitution? How and why did it come into existence? Just what, exactly, prompted the calling of the Constitutional Convention, which gave birth to it? Most Americans believe, logically enough, that after we sent His Britannic Majesty packing, it was time to create a new government. This is false, and it entirely overlooks the fact that we already had a functioning government at the time of the Convention. That government had been in effect for the entirety of the Revolution and for ***six years*** following the final British defeat at Yorktown.

No, the Convention was prompted by internal strife, by domestic corruption, oppression, and chaos, all but forgotten today, that had nothing to do with the departure of the British. That crisis revolved around a welfare program fed by the printing of paper money in some of the newly independent states.

We must be very clear on this point. Though you've probably never heard of it, the paper money crisis is ***the*** reason we have the Constitution. No other causal issue even comes close. The words of the Framers themselves, and even those of their opponents, the Anti-Federalists, demonstrate this beyond any doubt.

Before diving into the specifics of the paper-money crisis—and it ***was*** a crisis, one big enough to warrant the overthrow of one government in favor of another—we'll take a moment to look at welfare schemes in general, especially as they relate to democratic/representative governments.

Until now, I've avoided directly tackling the elephant in the room, that elephant being welfare spending. I've certainly discussed welfare spending when I mentioned multinational firms and special interest groups all bothering politicians to make sure that ***your*** money ends up in ***their*** pockets, but I've avoided the "W" word. No more. In this chapter, we will see that we owe the creation of our Constitution to the Framers' disgust and loathing of a traditional welfare program. It was welfare in its most basic form—a bunch of poor people wanted the money of a smaller group of wealthier people, so they, empowered by democracy, stole it. The Framers' revulsion at this state of affairs led them to make federal welfare programs unconstitutional.

[I cannot] undertake to lay [my] finger on that article in the Federal Constitution which granted a right to Congress of expending, on objects of benevolence, the money of their constituents.

— James Madison

(and he would certainly know, wouldn't he?)[73]

I cannot find any authority in the Constitution for making the federal government the great almoner of public charity throughout the United States. [Such spending] would, in my judgment, be contrary to the letter and the spirit of the Constitution, and subversive of the whole theory upon which the union of these States is founded.

— Franklin Pierce[74]

I feel obliged to withhold my approval of the plan... to indulge a benevolent and charitable sentiment through the appropriation of public funds.... I can find no warrant for such an appropriation in the Constitution.

— Grover Cleveland,

vetoing a bill to assist drought-stricken farmers[75]

Notice that Cleveland's fealty to true Constitutional principles led him to read that document in search of a specific grant of power allowing him to do something. He did not find it. Your cash stayed in your pocket.

Today's Bill of Rights approach—again, a perfect opposite of the Framers' approach—would have produced a perfectly opposite result, would have had Cleveland scanning the Constitution in search of specific language ***prohibiting*** him from spending your money. He would not find that language in the Bill of Rights. This is yet another shining example of the Bill of Very Few rights ***expanding*** government power and shrinking the sphere of personal freedom. Oh, and say goodbye to your cash.

Again, the simple yet profound difference between the Bill or Rights and the Enumeration cannot be overstated. Consulting the Bill of Rights to see how much money the feds can take from you leads inevitably to "***All*** of it." Doing the same with the Enumeration leads to "Almost none of it."

That this happened, (people using the government to legislate welfare for themselves) however, should come as no surprise. What did we learn from *Federalist* 10 in the previous chapter? It is property that divides society and drives the strife that makes government necessary. The Framers knew that the entire history of mankind was one long, sad saga in which those who rule—be they kings, aristocrats, or oligarchs, the many, the few, or the one—oppress those who are ruled.

As Madison noted, the oppression can and will take many forms, but, given that the unequal distribution of property is "the most common and durable" source of factional strife, we could easily guess what form this oppression would most often take.[76] As if Madison needed to tell us: the powerful rob the powerless.

And history, both ancient and the history that they were living at the time of the Convention, informed the Framers that a democratic/representative government, a government of "the people," without proper safeguards, would be no different.

> *Give all power to the many, they will oppress the few. Give all power to the few, they will oppress the many.*
>
> — Alexander Hamilton[77]

Yes, even under a democratic government, somebody rules and somebody's about to get robbed. So, who was in charge in America in 1787?

Well, that would be the people, the numerous poor, the common man…

And property drives strife…

And there were a lot more poor people than there were rich people…

See where this is going?

People, especially people with power, are not to be trusted. This does not change just because those in charge are the majority, the "common folk." Empowered people inevitably oppress those without power. In a democratic form of government, the rich minority will be powerless against the poor majority, and hence their property/money will be threatened.

And that's exactly what was happening in America in 1787 with paper money. And the reason the Constitutional Convention was called was because indebted farmers were using the power of democracy to steal money from their creditors.

> *Extend it [the vote] equally to all, and the rights of property or the claims of justice may be overruled by a majority without property or interested in measures of injustice. Of this abundant proof is afforded by other popular governments, and is not without examples in our own....*
>
> *In civilized communities, property as well as personal rights is an essential object of the laws, which encourage industry by securing the enjoyment of its fruits....*
>
> *In a just and a free Government, therefore, the rights both of property and of persons ought to be effectually guarded. Will the former be so in case of a universal and equal suffrage? Will the latter be so in case of a suffrage confined to the holders of property?*

> *...On the other hand, the danger to the holders of property cannot be disguised, if they be undefended against a majority without property.*
>
> — JAMES MADISON[78]

Yes, the Framers wrote the Constitution to safeguard against the chief defect of democratic/representative government—the oppression of the wealthy minority by the poor majority. This will become even more clear when we examine Article I, Section X of the Constitution.

But it goes way beyond merely protecting the wealthy from the poor, and that's because not every political question comes down to the rich versus the poor. Yesterday, today, or tomorrow, it could just as easily be 2,000 wealthy land barons versus 1,000 wealthy developers. That's the beauty of the thing—all legislative disputes will involve a minority and a majority, and each and every single constitutional hurdle or roadblock will be there for that minority group, making it more difficult for the empowered to steamroll the weak. Put another way, there is no constitutional provision that deploys, say, judicial review only for questions of rich versus poor.

Calling the Constitutional Convention

Here is Richard Henry Lee (or possibly Melancton Smith) writing as the Federal Farmer in opposition to the new federal government explaining why the Convention was called.

> Our governments have been new and unsettled; and several legislatures, by making tender, suspension, and paper money laws, have given just cause of uneasiness to creditors. By these and other causes, several orders of men in the community have been prepared, by degrees, for a change of government. And this very abuse of power in the legislatures, which in some cases has been charged upon the democratic part of the community, has furnished aristocratical men with those very weapons, and those very means, with which, in great measure, they are rapidly effecting their favourite object....
>
> The conduct of several legislatures, touching paper money, and tender laws, has prepared many honest men for changes in government, ***which otherwise they would not have thought of.***[79]

James Madison wrote "Vices of the Political System of the United States" just before the Convention for the same reason: to explain why the Convention was being called and to lay out the national political "vices" that made a new government necessary. He wrote of 12 different vices. Paper money, only one of the 12, took up 1,200 of the 3,100 words, more than any other subject. This was ***nearly three times the number of words*** dedicated to the next leading subject. Freedom of speech, worship, and the press were not mentioned even once.

Or, as the Colliers said,

> What concerned Madison most in "Vices" was not only that the states were flouting national regulations, but that they were treating unjustly certain minorities [the creditor class] within their own borders.
>
> ...Madison was especially troubled by the stay laws and tender laws and the paper money that so many of the plain people of the country were clamoring for. These laws, Madison believed, were "oppressing" the creditor minority.[80]

There is a very good reason Madison "believed" paper money laws were "oppressing" the creditor minority, and that's because paper money laws were oppressing the creditor minority. And yes, when the Framers speak of "the minority," they are most often speaking of the wealthy, and that's because it's all about money. As John Adams said, "The great art of law-giving consists in balancing the poor against the rich."[81]

Notice the quotation about the creditor minority above. It's not simply the age-old story of government favoring one group over another. It is more specific than that. It reflects what we've already noted as the central problem of a republican/democratic form of government—the less well-off majority using their power to take from the wealthy minority.

And the story of paper money reflects that perfectly. It is a simple tale of greed and corruption fueled by the power of democracy degenerating into oppression and turmoil. For the Framers, paper money was the manifestation of all their fears of mob rule and the chaos that comes with it. Yes, there were other issues and concerns, chiefly the tendency of the states to strangle interstate trade and the fear that the states might constantly war with each other, much like the European powers, or be weak in the face of foreign attack, but, other than the trade issue, these things were merely theoretical in nature, while paper money was all too real.

Without the impetus of the paper-money crisis, there simply would have been no convention in 1787. There just would have been no urgency in the states to bother with a convention lacking that critical spark.

As you read of paper money, you might wonder just exactly what the fuss was all about. After all, most of us have spent the entirety of our lives in a world where the feds spend staggering sums incomprehensible to the human mind on near numberless welfare programs.

When 50% of the federal budget is "income redistribution" of one form or another, the idea that the Framers would overthrow a government because of ***a single*** welfare scheme is surely inconceivable. But that is the fact of the matter, and it says all you need to know about the Framers' views on your paycheck.

Furthermore, "paper-money schemes could not stand on their own and necessarily spawned a whole series of additional laws, each one more odious than its predecessor, to prop up the whole corrupt edifice."[82]

"The Colliers tell us that the paper money crisis began when debtors, usually farmers struggling to make loan payments, would turn to their state legislatures and push for the creation of paper money. That was welfare pure and simple, as the paper money had nowhere near the worth of the gold, silver, or other medium of payment specified in original loan documents, and that, of course, was exactly the idea behind the legislation. Debtors also forced the creation of such extraordinary measures as 'stay laws,' which postponed or even *canceled* debt collection. Then there were the awful 'tender laws,' and 'ex post facto laws,' which actually compelled unwilling creditors to accept the newly printed paper money regardless of what the preexisting contract specified. Printing paper money was one thing, but to actually nullify preexisting contracts and force creditors to accept it in payment was simply more than the Framers could tolerate."[83]

Barring all these legislative efforts, armed farmer bands took to forcibly closing down sheriffs' auctions of debtors' property. They shut down and even burned courthouses, and finally, they fielded a rebel army that was quickly defeated in Massachusetts.

"But it was the example of Rhode Island that most horrified the Framers. The legislature, dominated by indebted farmers, circulated paper money that creditors naturally refused to accept. The legislature then made acceptance mandatory. Many creditors at this point actually fled the state to avoid the dreaded paper. The government's answer was simply to pass more corrupt legislation, this time allowing debtors to legally discharge the debt by depositing money with courts and posting an advertisement attesting to such in newspapers."[84]

For those who might think that the wealthy will always be fine and need no protections, this is a sobering tale. For the creditor class of Rhode Island, their wealth was powerless in the face of unchecked democracy. Again, they fled the state—***they actually left their homes***—and still the mob stole from them.

"Things got nastier still. When Rhode Island's supreme court declared the paper-money law unconstitutional, the legislature simply threw the court out of office and replaced the justices"[85] with, according to Madison, "willing instruments of the wicked and arbitrary plans of their masters."[86]

"Property rights aside, the Framers believed that the baneful effects of all the legislative chaos, the internal turmoil, and the international ridicule and disrepute generated threatened the very existence of the nation."[87] It was long past time to fix things.

The following citations, virtually all from Madison's *Notes of Debates in the Federal Convention of 1787*, demonstrate just how consumed the Framers were with stopping "the democratic part of the community" from using the power of democracy to gang up on the rich and take their property through the use of paper money.

Amazingly, again and again and again, we see from these citations that proposed legislative schemes, philosophies of representation, and existing political arrangements are all judged good or bad based almost solely on whether or not they had prevented, would likely lead to, or had already led to the creation of paper money.

The simple fact of the matter is that virtually every single time the Framers seek to find an example of something "evil" or "wicked" to be avoided, something they wish their Constitution to repress, they turn to paper money. Mentions of the rights with which we are today so obsessed are conspicuous only in their total absence.

We might want to note here that in the holy trinity[88] of constitutional writing, the absolutely indispensable explanatory guides to what is in the Constitution and why, the Framers' burning obsession with your money is as subtle as a blast furnace. It is simply impossible to read those documents without realizing that the Constitution is all about safeguarding your money.

The Framers on Paper Money

So frightening was the specter of paper money that Convention delegate George Read said that granting the federal government the power to issue it "would be as alarming as the mark of the Beast in Revelation."[89]

New Hampshire delegate John Langdon said he would "rather reject the whole plan" than see the federal government granted this power.[90]

> *He was persuaded there was a better chance for proper elections by the people, if divided into large districts, than by the state legislatures. Paper money had been issued by the latter, when the former were against it.*
>
> — James Madison,
> speaking of George Mason at the Convention[91]

He differed from gentlemen who thought that a choice by the people would be a better guard against bad measures than by the legislatures. A majority of the people in South Carolina were notoriously for paper money as a legal tender; the Legislature had refused to make it a legal tender. The reason was, that the latter had some sense of character and were restrained by that consideration.

— James Madison,
speaking of Charles Pinckney at the Convention[92]

The great evils complained of were, that the state legislatures ran into schemes of paper-money, etc., whenever solicited by the people, and sometimes without even the sanction of the people. Their influence, then, instead of checking a like propensity in the National Legislature, may be expected to promote it.

— James Madison[93]

Mr. Gerry insisted, that the commercial and moneyed interest would be more secure in the hands of the state legislatures than of the people at large. The former have more sense of character, and will be restrained by that from injustice. The people are for paper money, when the legislatures are against it.

— James Madison,
speaking of Elbridge Gerry at the Convention[94]

Speaking of a proposed federal veto power on all state laws that were contrary to the Constitution, Madison notes that during the Convention, Elbridge Gerry was generally against it, but that "He had no objection to authorize a negative to paper money, and similar measures."[95]

Give all power to the many, they will oppress the few. Give all power to the few, they will oppress the many. Both, therefore, ought to have the power, that each may defend itself against the other. To the want of this check we owe our paper-money instalment laws, etc.

— Alexander Hamilton[96]

The internal police, as it would be called and understood by the states, ought to be infringed in many cases, as in the case of paper money, and other tricks by which citizens of other states may be affected.

— Gouverneur Morris[97]

In Rhode Island, the judges who refused to execute an unconstitutional law [paper money law] were displaced; and others substituted, by the legislature, who would be the willing instruments of the wicked and arbitrary plans of their masters.

— James Madison[98]

Rhode Island is a full illustration of the insensibility to character produced by a participation of numbers, in dishonorable measures, and of the length to which a public body may carry wickedness and cabal.

— Nathaniel Gorham[99]

The check provided in the second branch [Senate] was not meant as a check on legislative usurpations of power, but on the abuse of lawful powers, on the propensity in the first branch to legislate too much, to run into projects of paper money and similar expedients.

— Gouverneur Morris[100]

Either bad laws will be pushed or not. On the latter supposition, no check will be wanted; on the former, a strong check will be necessary. And this is the proper supposition. Emissions of paper money, largesses to the people, a remission of debts, and similar measures, will at some times be popular, and will be pushed for that reason.

— Gouverneur Morris,
on the need of a strong judiciary
to check the legislature[101]

> *He had also known good produced by an apprehension of it [making less than a majority a quorum in both House and Senate]. He had known a paper emission prevented by that cause in Virginia.*
>
> — JAMES MADISON,
> SPEAKING OF GEORGE MASON AT THE CONVENTION[102]

> *He recited the history of paper emissions, and the perseverance of the legislative assemblies in repeating them, with all the distressing effects of such measures before their eyes.*
>
> — JAMES MADISON,
> SPEAKING OF GOUVERNEUR MORRIS AT THE CONVENTION[103]

Speculating that national legislators would thankfully not be driven by the same interests as their counterparts in the state governments, interests that had given rise to paper money, Madison notes that,

> There has not been any moment since the peace at which the representatives of the Union would have given an assent to paper money or any other measure of a kindred nature.[104]

So what did the Framers do to rectify this situation? Where is the constitutional salvation from the evil of paper money? Relief lies in Article I, Section X [appended at the end of this chapter]. It is in Section X that we find the relatively few things that ***state*** governments may not do."[105] And on that list, of course, we find abridging contracts, issuing paper money, or making anything but gold and silver legal in the discharge of debts. Simple, done, finished, end of story.

But there are amazing things, incredible things, hidden in Article I, Section X, things ***not*** stated, words ***not*** written, that reveal more about how the Framers viewed your money than just about anything else you could name.

To fully understand this, we must revisit our old friend, the Bill of Very Few Rights. We must also understand that until well into the 1900s, the Bill of Rights did not ***in any way*** apply to the states. The Bill of Rights restricted the federal government and the federal government alone. Period. After all, the first words of the First Amendment read, "***Congress*** shall make no law..."[106] If you find this unbelievable, and almost everybody does, Google will reveal the truth of the matter in well under five seconds.

"In other words, until after the Constitution was amended following the Civil War, the states had absolute power to engage in censorship, regulate the press, suppress free speech, or even establish a state-supported church, which, in fact, ***many of the states actually did***." At the time of the Revolution, for example, most of the colonies had tax-supported churches; all except Rhode Island imposed legal restrictions on various sects and penalties for dissenters, apostates, blasphemers and idolators were numerous and severe.'[107]"[108]

Furthermore, McDonald writes that these internal police powers left to the states were "nearly unlimited" and ***"were not affected by the***

subsequent adoption of the bill of rights."[109] McDonald notes that the states could "establish the mode and manner of religious worship and instruction, and they could levy taxes for the support of religion...[and] they could stifle dissent, stifle freedom of the press, of speech, of inquiry. They could regulate food, drink, and clothing."[110]

When we talk about regulating food, drink, and clothing, we are not talking about protecting the people from tainted meat, or ensuring that their woolens have a minimally acceptable percentage of wool. We are talking about sumptuary laws, defined by Britannica.com as:

> Any law designed to restrict excessive personal expenditures in the interest of preventing extravagance and luxury. The term denotes regulations restricting extravagance in food, drink, dress, and household equipment, usually on religious or moral grounds.[111]

Again, the U.S. Constitution, including the Bill of Rights, and Article I, Section X, did ***nothing*** to change any of that. The Framers did not lift a finger or write a syllable to alter that state of affairs, and the last state-established church in America didn't vanish until the 1830s.

Can there be a stronger statement about how the Framers viewed your money? Paper-money welfare? Not a chance. State-sponsored church? Not a problem.

Before leaving paper money, let's reexamine Madison from *Federalist* 10. In the previous chapter, we noted how the highlighted words came down to money, money, and money. Now we can be a bit more precise—these highlighted words actually come down to welfare, welfare, and welfare.

> A rage for *paper money*, for an *abolition of debts*, for an *equal division of property*, or for any other improper or wicked project, will be less apt to pervade the whole body of the union, than a particular member of it.[112]

Let's give John Adams the last words on welfare, shall we? The below passages are so perfect and so stunning I'll let them speak for themselves. Would it be terribly repetitive of me to alert you to the "frankly religious intensity" of the words to come?

Oh, and in case you're like those government men from *Raiders of the Lost Ark* and Sunday school just was not your thing, "the lamb committed..." is a biblical reference. In that Bible passage, the lamb is Jesus. And in Adam's words, the lamb is...money. Wow!

> *Property must be secured, or liberty cannot exist: but if unlimited, or unbalanced power of disposing property, be put into the hands of those who have no property, France will find, as we have found, the lamb committed to the custody of the wolf. In such a case, all the pathetic exhortations and addresses of the National Assembly to the people, to respect property, will be regarded no more than the warbles of the songsters of the forest. The great art of law-giving consists in balancing the poor against the rich in the legislature.*
>
> — John Adams[113]

Suppose a nation, rich and poor, high and low, ten millions in number, all assembled together; not more than one or two millions will have lands, houses, or any personal property; if we take into the account the women and children, or even if we leave them out of the question, a great majority of every nation is wholly destitute of property, except a small quantity of clothes, and a few trifles of other moveables. Would Mr. Nedham[114] be responsible that, if all were to be decided by a vote of the majority, the eight or nine millions who have no property would not think of usurping over the rights of the one or two millions who have? Property is surely a right of mankind as really as liberty. Perhaps, at first, prejudice, habit, shame, or fear, principle or religion, would restrain the poor from attacking the rich, and the idle from usurping on the industrious; but the time would not be long before courage and enterprise would come, and pretexts be invented by degrees, to countenance the majority in dividing all the property among them, or, at least in sharing it equally with its present possessors. Debts would be abolished, first; taxes laid heavy on the rich, and not at all on the others; and at last a downright equal division of everything be demanded, and voted. What would be the consequence of this? The idle, the vicious, the intemperate, would rush into the utmost extravagance of debauchery, sell and spend all their share, and then demand a new division of those who purchased from them. The moment the idea is admitted into society, that property is not as sacred as the laws of God, and that there is not a force of law and public justice to protect it, anarchy and tyranny commence. If "THOU SHALT NOT COVET," and "THOU SHALT NOT STEAL," were not commandments of Heaven, they must be made inviolable precepts in every society before it can be civilized or made free.[115]

U.S. Constitution Article I, Section X

Powers Denied to the States

No State shall enter into any Treaty, Alliance, or Confederation; grant Letters of Marque and Reprisal; coin Money; emit Bills of Credit; make any Thing but gold and silver Coin a Tender in Payment of Debts; pass any Bill of Attainder, ex post facto Law, or Law impairing the Obligation of Contracts, or grant any Title of Nobility.

No State shall, without the Consent of the Congress, lay any Imposts or Duties on Imports or Exports, except what may be absolutely necessary for executing its inspection Laws: and the net Produce of all Duties and Imposts, laid by any State on Imports or Exports, shall be for the Use of the Treasury of the United States; and all such Laws shall be subject to the Revision and Control of the Congress.

No State shall, without the Consent of Congress, lay any Duty of Tonnage, keep Troops, or Ships of War in time of Peace, enter into any Agreement or Compact with another State, or with a foreign Power, or engage in War, unless actually invaded, or in such imminent Danger as will not admit of delay.

CHAPTER FOUR

The Second Amendment

"THE BEST AND MOST EFFECTUAL WAY TO ENSLAVE"[116]

HERE ARE TWO arguments you've never before heard that obliterate the ludicrous idea that the feds are empowered to take your guns. They are the legal argument and the context argument. We'll take the legal one first, though I believe the context argument is even better.

Here we go…

Below is, as we noted in chapter 1, what virtually all Americans, including gun grabbers and gun lovers, erroneously believe about the federal government:

- The feds may take your money to create and fund a Department of Education because the Bill of Very Few Rights does not prohibit this.

- The feds may take your money and give it to any of your fellow citizens for virtually any reason (welfare especially) because the Bill of Very Few Rights does not prohibit this.
- The feds may take your money and force you into a bankrupt Ponzi retirement scheme because the Bill of Very Few Rights does not prohibit this.
- The feds may take your money and give it to politicians' friends to build museums because the Bill of Very Few Rights does not prohibit this.

Gun grabbers jump on to this chain of logic and say that the feds may take your guns because the Second Amendment does not prohibit this, reading, in effect, "Militias are acceptable."

Their thinking is logical, clear, and simple. They believe that the federal government may do anything not prohibited by the Bill of Very Few Rights; therefore, an amendment that reads "Militias are acceptable" does not in any way prevent the federal government from exercising the power that they already held to take your guns.

Logical, clear, and simple, but utterly false.[117] After reading chapter 1 we can spot the fatally false premise of that logic from a thousand miles away—hell, we can spot it from Mars. The Enumeration, the original and infinitely superior bill of rights, no more gave the feds the power to take your guns than it gave them the power to establish a church, suppress free speech, or regulate the length of your hair. There existed no power for the feds to take your guns before the Bill of Rights, and no such power exists after the Bill of Rights.

Sure, a constitutional amendment certainly ***could*** have changed that state of affairs, but one that, again, reads in effect "Militias are acceptable," ending with "the right of the people to keep and bear Arms, shall not be infringed," can never, in any way, be twisted to read, "This amendment gives to the feds a new power: the one to take your guns." Not even the most "creative" of our Supreme Court justices could pull ***that*** rabbit out of a hat.

In sum, we know that people were secure in their gun rights ***before*** the Bill of Very Few Rights, and an amendment that reads, "A well regulated Militia, being necessary to the security of a free State, the right of the people to keep and bear Arms, shall not be infringed,"[118] cannot possibly strip the people of those rights.

Now we turn to the vital and all-important context in which both the Constitution and the Bill of Very Few Rights were created. In case you skipped ahead after chapter 1 to read about your guns here, you might want to jump back to chapter 7 for a deeper dive into this important point about context.

These documents were written and presented to a people untrusting and fearful of the new federal government. We have here a context in which the Framers spent months writing dozens of essays and arguing before state ratifying conventions, promising the people that the new government would not be too powerful, would respect its limits, and would govern over only those matters where the Constitution gave it clear authority.

We have a context in which some Americans were so mistrustful of the new government that, even after ratification, they forced the creation of a bill of rights as ***a guarantee of individual liberty and an additional safeguard against federal power***. Nobody can plausibly argue that the Bill of Rights was created because those pushing for it wanted an ***expansion*** of federal power.

"Picture in your mind for a moment the rough-and-tumble individualist who gave birth to this nation, a man who had tamed a wilderness, fought Indian wars on and off for 180 years, and successfully faced down the world's mightiest empire. Hold a picture of that man in your head for a moment and then try to imagine his being told that this new federal government would have the power to regulate his ownership of firearms in any manner it saw fit, including imprisoning him for possession of any firearm for any reason at any time."[119]

No honest person could ever profess for even a second that the men who founded this nation would ***ever*** have submitted to such a thing, especially as, lacking any significant gun crime at the time, the only conceivable reason for such a federal power grab would be to lay the groundwork for subjugating the populace. Is it possible to imagine an innocent reason for the feds to disarm the people in 1790?

George Mason saw the obvious reason for grabbing our guns.

"When the resolution of enslaving America was formed in Great Britain, the British Parliament was advised...to disarm the people; that it was the best and most effectual way to enslave them."[120]

"To believe differently, to believe that the Second Amendment actually ***gives*** [emphasis added] the feds the authority to regulate firearms, one must believe the absolutely unbelievable. One must believe that the Anti-Federalists, fearing and loathing federal power, compelled Madison to compose this laundry list of rights, this list of things over which the government *was to have no authority* [emphasis in original],"[121] and that these people in fear of the federal government were just fine with an amendment that robbed them of their gun rights.

We must further believe that James Madison was such a monumentally incompetent and abysmal writer that, when trying to give the federal government this new authority to regulate the private ownership of firearms, the last fourteen words of the amendment read, 'The right of the people to keep and bear arms shall not be infringed.'

"We must also believe that revolutionary American history conceals some hitherto unknown and undocumented groundswell of public desire for gun control."[122]

The moment you understand that the Bill of Rights came into existence only at the insistence of and to satisfy those who were fearful and mistrustful of this new government is the moment debate and confusion must cease.

"There is simply no way on Earth the Anti-Federalists [or any other American in the 1780s] would have surrendered to the new and mistrusted government the right to own any gun they wanted at any time they wanted in any number they wanted."[123]

Context is everything. Most people are wrong about the backstory, the context, of the creation of the Bill of Rights, and it leads them astray. If you incorrectly believe, as I certainly used to, that the Founding Fathers/Framers sat down in secret meetings, in isolation, with no outside pressure, to write the Bill of Rights and Constitution because the Brits were gone and we needed a new government, and then you read the Second Amendment, it's actually pretty easy to be confused about that amendment.

And that's because your backstory/context is all wrong; it misidentifies both why and when the Bill of Rights was written, and it takes into account nobody other than the Framers. Those are fatal flaws. It leaves the all-important Anti-Federalists out of the picture. When looking at the Bill of Rights, the Framers are irrelevant, having as much to do with the Bill as did the Dallas Cowboys. It is the Anti-Federalists and the politician (Madison) who lost a Senate seat because of them who count.

So let's look at the ***real*** backstory, the ***real*** reason we have a bill of rights. This context ends the debate and ends the confusion.

The Framers write and the people ratify the Constitution. After ratification, ***those Americans most opposed to the federal government, most fearful and distrusting of it***, force Madison to write a bill of rights as an additional guarantee of individual liberty. ***Now*** do you thinks it's possible that that amendment gives the feds the authority to take your guns?

Fifty-seven words and the debate is over. Finished.

All of the points made above can be just as easily used to demonstrate the damage done by the Bill of Rights to original intent with other contested Constitutional provisions—the First Amendment and pornography, for instance. This time we'll take sides with what is usually seen as a left-leaning cause.

The host of my favorite podcast recently referenced her time as a Department of Justice attorney working on obscenity cases, wondering if the Framers had meant to include pornography under the word "speech."

Now, let's look at Hamilton in *Federalist* 84 as he sheds light on this issue by explaining why bills of rights are dangerous in a government of enumerated powers such as ours was before the Bill of Rights was so tragically misinterpreted.

> They [bills of rights] would contain various exceptions to powers which are not granted; and on this very account, would afford a colourable pretext to claim more than were granted. For why declare that things shall not be done, which there is no power to do? Why, for instance, should it be said, that the liberty of the press shall not be restrained, when no power is given by which restrictions may be imposed? I will not contend that such a provision would confer a regulating power; but it is evident that it would furnish, to men disposed to usurp, a plausible pretence for claiming that power. They might urge with a semblance of reason, that the constitution ought not to be charged with the absurdity of providing against the abuse of an authority, which was not given, and that

> the provision against restraining the liberty of the press afforded a clear implication, that a power to prescribe proper regulations concerning it, was intended to be vested in the national government.[124]

If that argument seems a bit far-fetched, a bit unlikely, all we have to do is examine, for mere moments, a few of the most famous words in the English language: "freedom of speech."

The mere occurrence of the word "speech" in the Bill of Rights has, for decade upon decade, created and then fed a debate about what "they" meant when "they" penned the word.

What, exactly, is "speech"? Does it cover lap dancing or pornography? How about a man holding a sign that says "F&*% the government!"? Is that speech? He's not talking. He's just holding a sign. What about burning a flag? A draft card? A president in effigy? Head scratch, head scratch. Oh, philosopher kings! What can it all mean?!

Allow me to definitively end the debate, right here, right now.

What Madison meant with the first amendment was "I'm going to outflank the Anti-Federalist leadership by pretending to amend the constitution that I wrote. The First Amendment means nothing, and changes nothing."

This leaves us with the Enumeration. Read it and identify that part giving the feds jurisdiction over anything in the preceding paragraphs. Again, no Bill of Rights means no debate, no confusion, and diminished federal power.

And remember the context argument: nobody in the separate states had a desire, a need, or even a glimmer of a thought of the feds coming in and taking their cash to hire DOJ attorneys to ponder the meaning of "speech" or the definition of "obscenity," and then to report back with demands about what their laws should be.

How much time and how much of your money have been wasted on this debate, a debate created by the Bill of Very Few Rights?

CHAPTER FIVE

Human Nature and Democracy

"IMPULSES OF RAGE"[125]

LET'S TAKE A moment to see what a few of the Framers/Founders had to say about the closely related subjects of democracies, republics, majority rule, and human nature.

The Framers did not trust people in power—***any people***. As we've already seen, this includes the common man. He, like any other demographic you could name, not only wants to keep all of his cash, which is fine, but he pretty much wants all of yours, too, and will use government force to steal it. And as you will see below, the Framers were no fans of aristocrats or the elite, either.

This lack of trust ruled out any possibility of the Framers creating a democracy. They instead gave us a republic. Despite this antimajoritarian distinction and myriad other antimajoritarian constitutional measures (much more on these measures later), it was still the people, the common man, who would wield the lion's share of political power and who were ultimately in charge.

The Framers' dim view of human nature—not entirely bleak, or republican government would be impossible—complicated things. Merely rejecting monarchy, handing the people the reins, expanding the franchise, and relying on simple majority rule were just never gonna cut it.

After all, if man is wise, just, benevolent, and capable enough to wield the awesome, coercive force of government, ***why is government necessary at all***? It soon becomes apparent that it is man's nature that at once makes government necessary and makes man unfit to govern.

> *It may be a reflection on human nature, that such devices [checks and balances] should be necessary to control the abuses of government. But what is government itself, but the greatest of all reflections on human nature? If men were angels, no government would be necessary. If angels were to govern men, neither external or internal controls on government would be necessary.*
>
> — James Madison[126]

> *If Socrates and Plato, Cicero and Seneca, Hutcheson and Butler are to be credited, reason is rightfully supreme in man, and, therefore, it would be most suitable to the reason of*

mankind to have no civil or political government at all. The moral government of God, and his viceregent, Conscience, ought to be sufficient to restrain men to obedience, to justice, and benevolence, at all times and in all places; we must therefore descend from the dignity of our nature, when we think of civil government at all.

— John Adams[127]

An excellent writer has said, somewhat incautiously, that "a people will never oppress themselves, or invade their own rights." This compliment, if applied to human nature, or mankind, or to any nation or people, in being or in memory, is more than has been merited....

... "The people never think of usurping over other men's rights." What can this mean? Does it mean that the people never unanimously think of usurping over other men's rights? This would be trifling, for there would, by the supposition, be no other men's rights to usurp. But if the people never, jointly, nor severally, think of usurping the rights of others, what occasion can there be for any government at all?...

.... The proposition of our author then should be reversed, and it should have been said, that they mind so much their own, that they never think enough of others.

— John Adams[128]

For the Framers, this was the great paradox to be answered, the huge challenge to be met. History had shown clearly enough that neither kings, nor enlightened, cultured, educated aristocrats were to be trusted with government power. But how far could the people be trusted? Who is this creature, man? What is his nature? What, exactly, are these flaws that render him unfit to hold power over others? Before basing a government on humanity, better to determine what humanity is. Today especially, in our poll-driven world where majority desire is almost always equated with legitimacy, it might be instructive to see what the Framers thought of our desires.

By happy coincidence, when one examines and judges human nature, one is similarly evaluating democracy and majority rule. For obviously, whatever is good or lacking in man, whatever may be his proclivities, tendencies, or abilities, such will be the same with democracy. In the following quotations, therefore, the words "democracy," "man," "the majority," and references to single, popularly elected legislatures, are largely interchangeable.

Listing human failings is a task very simple in nature, but perhaps daunting in length. Any one of us who has ever read a history book or even today's headlines will be intimately familiar with man's dark side.

And while many Americans know something of the Framers' less than exalted view of human nature and of their doubts about human capacity for governing, few, perhaps, are aware of just how passionately and deeply held these views were, and how these views inform virtually every article and every clause of our Constitution.

People Are Bad...

The Framers were no strangers to human ugliness and described it in frank detail.

> *In the institution of government, it must be remembered, that although reason ought always to govern individuals, it certainly never did since the Fall, and never will till the Millennium; and human nature must be taken as it is, as it has been, and will be.*
>
> — John Adams[129]

> *It is weakness rather than wickedness which renders men unfit to be trusted with unlimited power.... The love of gold grows faster than the heap of acquisition; the love of praise increases by every gratification, till it stings like an adder, and bites like a serpent; till the man is miserable every moment when he does not snuff the incense: ambition strengthens at every advance, and at last takes possession of the whole soul so absolutely, that a man sees nothing in world of importance to others, or himself, but in his object.*
>
> — John Adams[130]

Human beings...are generally governed by rather base and selfish motives, by suspicion, jealousy, desire for self-aggrandizement, and disinclination to do more than is required by convenience or self-interest, or exacted of them by force.

— Edward McNall Burns,
paraphrasing James Madison[131]

Mankind are governed more by their feelings than by reason.

— Samuel Adams[132]

Take mankind in general they are vicious...One great error is, that we suppose mankind more honest than they are.

— Alexander Hamilton[133]

To judge from the history of mankind, we shall be compelled to conclude, that the fiery and destructive passions of war reign in the human breast with much more powerful sway, than the mild and beneficent sentiments of peace; and that to model our political systems upon speculations of lasting tranquility, would be to calculate on the weaker springs of the human character.

— Alexander Hamilton[134]

To presume a want of motives for such contests [internal strife], as an argument against their existence, would be to forget that men are ambitious, vindictive, and rapacious....

...Has it not, on the contrary, invariably been found, that momentary passions, and immediate interests, have a more active and imperious control over human conduct, than general or remote considerations of policy, utility, or justice? Have republics in practice been less addicted to war than monarchies? Are not the former administered by men as well as the latter?

— Alexander Hamilton[135]

Free government is founded on jealousy and not in confidence...in questions of power then, let no more be heard of confidence in man, but bind him down from mischief by the chains of the constitution.

— Thomas Jefferson[136]

And speaking of man's political heritage in *Federalist* 37, Madison observes that it was little more than "a history of factions, contentions, and disappointments; and may be classed among the most dark and degrading pictures, which display the infirmities and depravities of the human character."[137]

Very well, critics might argue, anybody may refer to a dictionary and a criminal code to compile a list of negative adjectives and violent or felonious acts. To recognize that some are capable of evil is not an indictment against mankind in general or his ability to govern, some might say.

But it is ***not*** the sins and transgressions of a tiny minority of sociopaths or violent criminals that make government necessary. It is instead man in general and man in groups who, throughout history, inevitably falls to murder and violence, anarchy and chaos in the absence of government. And if we were to wave away the more overt and violent sins of man, we would still be left with the less obvious, less destructive flaws—the selfish, petty, mean, cheap, and avaricious actions of a ***majority*** of people, who very likely are model citizens ***most*** of the time.

> *Is not a great part, I will not say the greatest part, of men detected every day in some disposition or other, stronger or weaker, more or less, to usurp over other men's rights?...If we should extend our candour so far as to own that the majority of men are generally under the dominion of benevolence and good intentions, yet it must be confessed that a vast majority frequently transgress; and, what is more directly to the point, not only a majority, but almost all, confine their benevolence to their families, relations, personal friends, parish, village, city, county, province, and that very few indeed, extend it impartially to the whole community.*
>
> — JOHN ADAMS[138]

> *Indolence is the natural character of man, to such a degree, that nothing but the necessities of hunger, thirst, and other wants equally pressing, can stimulate him to action, until education is introduced in civilized societies, and the strongest motives of ambition to excel in arts, trades, and professions, are established in the minds of all men: until this emulation is introduced, the lazy savage holds property in too little estimation to give himself trouble for the preservation or acquisition of it.*
>
> — JOHN ADAMS[139]

> *Though we allow benevolence and generous affections to exist in the human breast, yet every moral theorist will allow the selfish passions in the generality of men to be the strongest.*
>
> — JOHN ADAMS[140]

People in Groups Are Really Bad…

But what of men operating within a political framework? Would not some of the bad in human nature be diminished or eliminated after having been filtered through a political process? We certainly expect some people to be wholly self-interested and utterly unconcerned with truth, morality, or anything but securing their own ends, but what of the legislatures, the executives, or the judiciaries in democratic nations? Can legitimate democratic governments consistently produce outcomes that resemble less the rule of law than the desires of the anarchistic mobs that government is instituted to control?

Or, as asked by Alexander Hamilton in *Federalist* 15, "Has it been found that bodies of men act with more rectitude or greater disinterestedness than individuals?"[141]

Unfortunately, the exact opposite is true; men acting in groups are actually worse. One of our most specific and troubling failings is our readiness, indeed eagerness, to oppress unpopular minorities, and even more frightening is our tendency to this oppression while in concert with large groups, such as within a political system or a mob—the two can be remarkably similar.

Another major philosophical influence on the Framers was David Hume, the 18th century Scottish philosopher who wrote that man's propensity to oppress his fellow man was directly related to his association with groups.[142]

Very few of us would ever jump on the soapbox and demand that the government steal from our wealthier neighbors and transfer the cash to us. But when we round the corner and see 300 of our peers demanding the same thing? Well, it's far easier to join the mob than to start or lead it. This is especially true with political groups. One of the single worst things about government systems is that decisions arrived at after going through them give just about ***anything*** a patina of legitimacy. This is especially true if we're talking about a democracy or a republic, or if we're talking about government seizing your dirty, filthy money, which, as noted earlier, certainly doesn't come close to having anything to do with your sacred rights now, does it?

Or, according to the masters,

We well know, that neither moral nor religious motives can be relied on as an adequate control [of "the majority"]. They are not found to be such on the injustice and violence of individuals ***and lose their efficacy in proportion to the number combined together; that is, in proportion as their efficacy becomes needful.***

— James Madison[143]

Why has government been instituted at all? Because the passions of men will not conform to the dictates or reason and justice, without constraint. Has it been found that bodies of men act with more rectitude or greater disinterestedness than individuals? The contrary of this has been inferred by all accurate observers of the conduct of mankind; and the inference is founded upon obvious reasons. Regard to reputation, has a less active influence, when the infamy of a bad action is to be divided among a number, than when it is to fall singly upon one. A spirit of faction, which is apt to mingle its poison in the deliberations of all bodies of men, will often hurry the persons, of whom they are composed, into improprieties and excesses, for which they would blush in a private capacity.

— Alexander Hamilton[144]

It is no less true, that the strength of opinion in each individual, and its practical influence on his conduct, depend much on the number which he supposes to have entertained the same opinion. The reason of man, like man himself, is timid and cautious when left alone; and acquires firmness and confidence, in proportion to the number with which it is associated.

— James Madison[145]

A prudent regard to the maxim that honesty is the best policy is found by experience to be as little regarded by bodies of men as by individuals. Respect for character is always diminished in proportion to the number among whom the blame or praise is to be divided. Conscience, the only remaining tie, is known to be inadequate in individuals: In large numbers, little is to be expected from it.

— James Madison[146]

Bodies of men are not less swayed by interest than individuals, and are less controlled by the dread of reproach and the other motives felt by individuals.

— James Madison[147]

In other words, groups, certainly including "the majority," do not vote for what is right or just—***they vote for what they want***.

That the desires of the majority of the people are often for injustice and inhumanity against the minority, is demonstrated by every page of the history of the whole world.

— JOHN ADAMS[148]

On a candid examination of history, we shall find that turbulence, violence, and abuse of power, by the majority trampling on the rights of the minority, have produced factions and commotions, which, in republics, have, more frequently than any other cause, produced despotism.

— JAMES MADISON[149]

In all cases where a majority are united by a common interest or passion, the rights of the minority are in danger.

— JAMES MADISON[150]

Now grant but this truth, and the question is decided: if a majority are capable of preferring their own private interest, or that of their families, counties, and party, to that of the nation collectively, some provision must be made in the constitution, in favor of justice, to compel all to respect the common right, the public good, the universal law, in preference to all private and partial considerations.

— JOHN ADAMS[151]

Therefore, Democracy Is…Well, You Know

Democracy—the very word gave the Framers nightmares. For them, democracy was the mindless, not-quite-human violence of the mob and nothing else. It led inevitably to chaos, and then to anarchy, and then to iron-fisted tyranny.

> *Democracy never lasts long. It soon wastes, exhausts, and murders itself. There never was a democracy yet that did not commit suicide.*
>
> — JOHN ADAMS[152]

But what did "democracy" mean to the Framers? This is an important question because there are many definitions and degrees of democracy. In the broad sense, democracy was simply any government where the people, the common man, the majority, reigned supreme with unchecked power. The word is often used in the classical Greek sense, meaning a single assembly of eligible electorate, physically gathering to debate and vote on all questions of government. There was no selecting of representatives to be sent to a distant capitol to wrestle with the questions of state on behalf of the citizen.

Greek-like democracy was never a consideration for the Framers, so when they use the word they generally mean democracy as it was practiced in America in the 1700s. So, yes, representatives were chosen, but too often this still meant unchecked majority rule and ***lots*** of control by the people. This was not good. In fact, it was too much democracy that led to the paper-money crisis that birthed the Constitution. Simple democracy dictated that farmers, a huge majority, got what they wanted, when they wanted it. Creditors, a tiny minority, were legally robbed at the point of a government gun.

The evils we experience flow from the excess of democracy.

— Elbridge Gerry[153]

The general object [of the convention] was to provide a cure for the evils under which the U.S. labored; that, in tracing these evils to their origin, every man had found it in the turbulence and follies of democracy.

— Edmund Randolph[154]

The instability, injustice, and confusion, introduced into the public councils, have, in truth, been the mortal diseases under which popular governments have every where perished.... Complaints are every where heard from our most considerate and virtuous citizens...[that] the public good is disregarded in the conflicts of rival parties; and that measures are too often decided, not according to the rules of justice, and the rights of the minor party, but by the superior force of an interested and overbearing majority....

From this view of the subject, it may be concluded that a pure democracy, by which I mean, a society consisting of a small number of citizens, who assemble and administer the government in person, can admit of no cure for the mischiefs of faction. A common passion or interest will, in almost every case, be felt by a majority of the whole; a communication and concert, results from the form of government itself; and there is nothing to check the inducements to sacrifice the weaker party, or an obnoxious individual. Hence it is, that such democracies have ever been spectacles of turbulence and contention; have ever been found incompatible with personal security, or the rights of property; and have, in general, been as short in their lives, as they have been violent in their deaths.

— James Madison[155]

I was always for a Free Republic; not a Democracy, which is as arbitrary Tyrannical, bloody cruel and intolera[nt] a Government as that of Phalaris with his Bull is represented to have been.

— John Adams[156]

Speaking of the defects he found in Thomas Paine's plan for government, laid out in *Common Sense*, John Adams said it,

---

was so democratical, without any restraints or even an attempt at any equilibrium or counterpoise, that it must produce confusion and every evil work.

— Autobiography of John Adams[157]

The voice of the people has been said to be the voice of God; and however generally this maxim has been quoted and believed, it is not true in fact. The people are turbulent and changing; they seldom judge or determine right.

— Alexander Hamilton[158]

Are not popular assemblies frequently subject to the impulses of rage, resentment, jealousy, avarice, and of other irregular and violent propensities? Is it not well known, that their determinations are often governed by a few individuals in whom they place confidence, and that they are of course liable to be tinctured by the passions and views of those individuals?

— Alexander Hamilton[159]

Wherever there is an interest and power to do wrong, wrong will generally be done, and not less readily by a powerful and interested party than by a powerful and interested prince.

— James Madison[160]

As noted earlier, it would be a mistake to read the words above and see the Framers or Founders as trusting in the elites or aristocrats, staring down their noses at their supposed inferiors. Such a thing would be virtually impossible—these men, after all, could and did read history once in a while, and it would require a breathtaking ignorance of that history, combined with some world-class feeble-mindedness, to actually go around believing that aristocrats were some sort of angelic, elevated people who just would not dream of oppressing the powerless.

It is very easy to flatter the democratical proportion of society, by making such distinctions between them and the monarchical and aristocratical; but flattery is as base an artifice, and as pernicious a vice, when offered to the people, as when given to the others. There is no reason to believe the one much honester or wiser than the other; they are all of the same clay, their minds and bodies are alike. The two latter have more knowledge and sagacity derived from education, and more advantages for acquiring wisdom and virtue. As to usurping others' rights, they are all three equally guilty when unlimited in power: no wise man will trust either with an opportunity; and every judicious legislator will set all three to watch and control each other.

— John Adams[161]

And never let Adams near a pen if he's going to attack you…

I often laugh at it too, for there is nothing in this laughable world more ridiculous than the management of it [aristocracy] by all the nations of the earth; but while we smile, mankind have reason to say to us, as the frogs said to the boys, what is sport to you, are wounds and death to us.

> *When I consider the weakness, the folly, the pride, the vanity, the selfishness, the artifice, the low craft and mean cunning, the want of principle, the avarice, the unbounded ambition, the unfeeling cruelty of a majority of those (in all nations) who are allowed an aristocratical influence, and, on the other hand, the stupidity with which the more numerous multitude not only become their dupes, but even love to be taken in by their tricks, I feel a stronger disposition to weep at their destiny than to laugh at their folly.*
>
> — John Adams[162]

Still, critics will note that the Framers/Founders spilled far more ink detailing the failings of the common man than those of the elites. The obvious reason for that is that the Framers were creating a republican form of government, one in which the people were to wield the greatest power. It was the people, therefore, who needed to be most clearly understood, most carefully watched, and most heavily shackled.

As we shall see, the Framers find a way around this mistrust of all who would administer the affairs of state, and are able to lay out a plan for legitimate, representative government.

CHAPTER SIX

Protecting the Minority

"SUDDEN AND VIOLENT PASSIONS"[163]

Aristocrats, the elite, the common man, the majority, democracy—bad, bad, bad. All bad. What are we gonna do about this? How are we to craft good representative government that respects rights and protects people when this is the clay with which we must work?

This is where those famous checks and balances come into play. Famous, indeed, but nearly as misunderstood as the Bill of Rights.

Before getting to the specifics of checks and balances, let us look at them in the broadest terms. People believe that the House can check the Senate and the Senate can check the House. Or it could be the president checking the House, or the Senate checking the president, and so on.

You might have noticed that what is being checked in all those examples is the very government that the Framers created. And that is the broad point that we must first address.

Many have noted over the years that this system of protection is essentially negative in its view of people and government—the Constitution did ***not*** create a government empowered to protect you.

Relying on government, or whatever people or faction happen to be in power at any given time, to look out for and protect the powerless would be to place faith in what Hamilton called the "weaker springs of the human character."[164]

The Framers would not make that mistake. No, the strategy behind the Constitution was to create a federal government that was, at least on the domestic front, handcuffed, restrained, and ***too weak to hurt you***.

As we continue in this chapter, you will notice that negativity over and over again—it is never about government doing good and securing rights. It is always about a restrained government blocked from doing bad.

Another mistaken belief about checks and balances—and it is here where we find the hugest of misconceptions—is that these measures exist to check politicians or the hazy and undefined "government power." In other words, we believe that they exist to ensure that a bunch of congressmen bent on a scheme to rob the people of their rights are "checked" by a bunch of equally powerful senators or vice versa. This is completely false.

Checks and balances are designed almost entirely to check the will of the people, the majority. They are crafted to thwart legislators who are actually doing the peoples' bidding, ***legislators who are doing no more than simply trying to give to the people what it is that they want.***

In our governments the real power lies in the majority of the community, and the invasion of private rights is chiefly to be apprehended, not from acts of government contrary to the sense of its constituents, but from acts in which the government is the mere instrument of the major number of the constituents. This is a truth of great importance, but not yet sufficiently attended to.

— James Madison[165]

The check provided in the second branch [Senate] was not meant as a check on legislative usurpations of power, but on the abuse of lawful powers, on the propensity of the first branch to legislate too much to run into projects of paper-money,[166] and similar expedients.

— Gouverneur Morris[167]

Read the words above. The "majority," who want to steal the minority's money, are the problem, and the Senate exists to check the House, an instrument of the majority. We see the exact same thing in the next two quotations.

And if the people are sufficiently enlightened to see all the dangers that surround them, they will always be represented by a distinct personage to manage the whole executive power; a distinct senate, to be guardians of property against levellers[168] for the purposes of plunder.

— John Adams[169]

Government is instituted no less for the protection of property, than of the persons of individuals. The one, as well as the other, therefore, may be considered as represented by those who are charged with the government. Upon this principle it is, that in several of the states, and particularly in the state of New York, one branch of the government is intended more especially to be the guardian of property, and is accordingly elected by that part of society which is most interested in this object of government.

— James Madison[170]

One might think that the House is also meant as a check on the Senate, that this is a two-way street. But that's not really the case. It is the "republican principle" that not only empowers the people but simultaneously provides all the check one needs on the elite and "their" Senate.

> *If a faction consists of less than a majority, relief [from oppression] is supplied by the republican principle, which enables the majority to defeat its sinister views, by regular vote.*
>
> — James Madison[171]

What is really being checked are the common people, those who have the most power under our Constitution. Indeed, after empowering the people by leaving their democratic/republican state governments in place, the Constitution spends the next 4,000 or so words clawing back that grant of power.

The entire thrust of the Constitution—indeed, the very reason for its existence—is the control of the majority, the protection of minority groups and interests. Virtually the whole of the Constitution is a monument to the employ of checks and balances for the protection of the minority from what John Adams called the "wicked" majority.[172]

The people, the ultimate holders of power in a republic, then, were to be denied the power and ability to do to others the very things that those who held political power had always done—oppress the powerless and rob them of their natural rights.

This should not be at all surprising, given what we've read to this point. Remember:

- Those in power oppress those without.
- Through the Constitution, the Framers left political power to the common man.
- Therefore, the common man must be checked.

Now let's get a bit more specific with our checks and balances. We've already discussed the Enumeration—a significant check and balance, the original bill of rights, the all-important beating heart of the Constitution that flat-out makes it illegal for the government to simply go about handing your cash to anybody on planet Earth for any reason whatsoever at any time whatsoever. But there is a problem with the Enumeration, and we'll call it the "parchment barrier" problem.

> *Experience proves the inefficacy of a bill of rights on those occasions when its control is most needed. Repeated violations of these parchment barriers have been committed by overbearing majorities in every state.*
>
> — James Madison[173]

Sadly, people who want your cash and have the power to steal it are not always deterred by something as trifling as the law or by a list on a piece of paper under glass somewhere in Washington, DC. No, the Enumeration cannot stand on its own; there must be some constitutional mechanisms to give it force, some checks and balances. One of the most important of those mechanisms (federalism is another big one) is a bicameral legislature.

The bicameral legislature is a very simple thing. The House belongs to the people—all of the electorate votes on the entire House every two years. The Senate belongs to the elite, the money men, the elder statesmen, the aristoi—call them what you wish, but when the people clamor for the wealthy's money, the Senate stands in the way. Of course, it ***used*** to be that way—constitutional amendments ensure the Senate and House have almost the same electorate. If not for the staggering of elections, the electorate would be entirely the same.

That is why a bicameral legislature works. Rights are protected here not because a senator wants to stop a representative simply because they belong to different components of the same government—the senator stops the representative because the people to whom the senator answers have radically different political desires than those who elected the representative. The Senate does not check the House—the Senate's ***constituents*** check the House's ***constituents***.

Thomas Jefferson's words below are all you need to know on the subject. He is speaking on the defects of the Virginia Constitution:

> The senate is, by its constitution, too homogenous with the house of delegates. Being chosen by the same electors, at the same time, and out of the same subjects, the choice falls of course on men of the same description. The purpose of establishing different houses of legislation is to

introduce the influence of different interests or different principles.[174]

Madison's thoughts on the subject are also, of course, worthy of your time. Note that he is speaking to the people here in *The Federalist Papers*, having the courage to actually tell the electorate who he hopes will ratify his constitution that they cannot always be trusted to do what is right. No politician would dare write these words today.

The necessity of a senate is not less indicated by the propensity of all single and numerous assemblies, to yield to the impulse of sudden and violent passions, and to be seduced by factious leaders into intemperate and pernicious resolutions. Examples on this subject might be cited without number; and from proceedings within the United States, as well as from the history of other nations. But a position that will not be contradicted, need not be proved.

— Federalist 62[175]

Such an institution [the Senate] may be sometimes necessary as a defense to the people against their own temporary errors and delusions.

— Federalist 63[176]

More from Adams below—he ***really*** didn't like single assemblies/simple democracy/majority rule.

> *Of all the possible forms of government, a sovereignty in one assembly, successively chosen by the people, is, perhaps, the best calculated to facilitate the gratification of self-love, and the pursuit of the private interests of a few individuals. A few eminent, conspicuous characters will be continued in their seats in the sovereign assembly, from one election to another, whatever changes are made in the seats around them. By superior art, address, and opulence, by more splendid birth, reputations, and connections, they will be able to intrigue with their people, and their leaders out of doors, until they worm out most of their opposers and introduce their friends. To this end they will bestow all offices, contracts, privileges in commerce, and other emoluments on the latter, and their connections, and throw every vexation and disappointment in the way of the former, until they establish such a system of hopes and fears throughout the State as shall enable them to carry a majority in every fresh election of the house. The judges will be appointed by them and their party, and of consequence will be obsequious enough to their inclinations. The whole judicial authority, as well as the executive, will be employed, perverted, and prostituted to the purpose of electioneering. No justice will be obtainable, nor will innocence or virtue be safe in the judicial courts but for the friends of the prevailing leaders. Legal prosecutions will be instituted and carried on against opposers, to their vexation*

and ruin. And as they have the public purse at command, as well as the executive and judicial power, the public money will be expended in the same way.

— COMMENTARIES ON THE CONSTITUTION OF THE UNITED STATES[177]

I think a people cannot be long free, nor ever happy, whose government is in one assembly. My reasons for this are as follow:

1. A single assembly is liable to all the vices, follies, and frailties of an individual; subject to fits of humor, starts of passion, flights of enthusiasm, partialities, or prejudice, and consequently productive of hasty results and absurd judgements. And all these errors ought to be corrected and defects supplied by some controlling power.

— "THOUGHTS ON GOVERNMENT"[178]

They [man] know each other's imbecility so well, that they ought never to lead one another into temptation.... But who would trust his life, liberty, and property to a madman or an assembly of them? It would be safer to confide in knaves. Five hundred or five thousand together in an assembly are not less liable to this extravagance than one. The nation that commits its affairs to a single assembly, will assuredly find that its passions and desires augment as fast as those of a king. And therefore, a constitution with a single assembly must be essentially defective.

— "OPINIONS OF PHILOSOPHERS"[179]

A marginal notation in Adams's original copy of the "Opinions of Philosophers" quote reads "The majority are wicked."

Even if everybody votes and all viewpoints are heard, single assemblies are still bad. Here's your congressional district at the time of the Revolution:

1. Farmers: 100 voters
2. Tradesmen: 20 voters
3. Dockworkers: 10 voters
4. Creditors: 5 voters

Oversimplified, but you get the point. What happens if groups 2, 3, or 4 seek their congressman's aid in stealing from group 1? Well, unless their congressman is so poor at counting he needs to take off his gloves, socks, and pants to get to 11, ***nothing*** happens. Now what if group 1 wants to oppress, oh, I don't know, let's just be crazy for a moment and say group 4? By now, we all know the answer. All the creditors get to vote, but that won't do them any good.

A quick word about gridlock, that unholy terror that we hear so much about today. In case it's not been made clear, gridlock was demanded, required, desired, and expected by the men who wrote the Constitution. Nobody thought that the empowering of different and competing factions was going to produce anything but gridlock.

Our government was to be hobbled and restrained, and its power was to be checked at every turn. Ours is a government purposefully and knowingly designed to block and kill legislation, to be inefficient, slow, and unproductive. In all their words, we see the Framers repeat the same theme again and again: how to ensure that government won't do this, that the electorate won't do that, that Faction A will fail to enact an agenda, that Faction B will similarly be foiled. When you look at Adams, Madison, Jefferson, Washington, and all the rest, you will search in vain for thoughts or ideas on how to ensure that virtuous legislation, the good stuff, makes it through the system.

In the legislature, promptitude of decision is oftener an evil than a benefit. The differences of opinion, and the jarrings of parties in that department of the government, though they may sometimes obstruct salutary plans, yet often promote deliberation and circumspection; and serve to check excesses in the majority.

— Alexander Hamilton[180]

It may perhaps be said that the power of preventing bad laws includes that of preventing good ones; and may be used to the one purpose as well as to the other. But this objection will have little weight with those who can properly estimate the mischiefs of that inconstancy and mutability in the laws, which form the greatest blemish in the character and genius of our governments. They will consider every institution calculated to restrain the excess of law-making, and to keep things in the same state in which they happen to be at any given period, as much more likely to do good than harm;

> *because it is favourable to greater stability in the system of legislation. The injury which may possibly be done by defeating a few good laws, will be amply compensated by the advantage of preventing a number of bad ones.*
>
> — Alexander Hamilton[181]

All this is logically consistent with the notions that man has many rights, that the existence of government is a compromise, and that government is a flawed and inefficient organ of force and coercion tasked with protecting those rights. Such a situation naturally suggests that where government is concerned, one has something that must be watched and closely monitored, not empowered and turned loose in the hopes that it will do good.

Or, as the Colliers wrote,

> It [Madison's constitutional plan] is a plan for government that is essentially negative in its purpose. . . . Everything in Madison's plan was meant to curtail, contain, constrain power wherever it might lie.[182]

CHAPTER SEVEN

The Nature of Government

"THE JAWS OF POWER"[183]

HAVING SEEN THE Framers' views on human nature, we can easily guess what they thought of government in general. If man is avaricious, if he cannot be trusted and is often on the prowl for the power, property, and freedom of others, and if government, an institution of man, has a long, sad history of violence and oppression, then what could have been the Framers' expectations of government?

Were we directed from Washington when to sow, and when to reap, we should soon want bread.

— THOMAS JEFFERSON[184]

Society in every state is a blessing, but government even in its best state is but a necessary evil; in its worst state an intolerable one.

— Thomas Paine[185]

I own, I am not a friend to a very energetic government. It is always oppressive. It places the governors indeed more at their ease, at the expense of the people.... And say, finally, whether peace is best preserved by giving energy to the government, or information to the people. This last is the most certain, and the most legitimate engine of government.

— Thomas Jefferson[186]

The natural progress of things is for liberty to yield and for government to gain ground.

— Thomas Jefferson[187]

The jaws of power are always opened to devour, and her arm is always stretched out, if possible, to destroy the freedom of thinking, speaking, and writing.

— John Adams[188]

The legitimate powers of government extend to such acts only as are injurious to others.

— Thomas Jefferson[189]

Government is instituted to protect property of every sort; as well that which lies in the various rights of individuals, as that which the term particularly expresses. This being the end of government, that alone is a just government which impartially secures to every man whatever is his own.

— James Madison[190]

Look at those last two quotations. I often speak to people who ask, in one form or another, "Why must government do no more? What is so terrible about government simply trying to help people?"

Why cannot government legitimately go around actively helping its citizens, brightening their lives, doing everything in its power to make them better people, and improving their prospects emotionally, socially, and financially? Why cannot government actively help, rather than merely referee and ensure that predators are controlled?

The answer to that question is simple and can be fully stated in just a few words—government has but one way to help people, and that is through the forceful redistribution of the very property that it is instituted to protect. Never has there been found a way that government may help one person without necessarily violating the natural rights of another innocent party, beyond protecting its citizens from coercion and force.

Now, the words above might not be absolutely true 100% of the time. If you think hard enough, you might remember a truly cost-free government assistance program. But even the most benign-sounding proposals turn out not to be so benign after the most cursory of examinations.

Targeted tax breaks, especially those targeted at the poor, sound harmless enough, but every single dollar not paid in taxes by a poor person must necessarily be paid by somebody else. Enterprise Zones sound really good, but those "tax concessions," again, must be paid by others. It goes without saying, of course, that "corporate welfare" carries the same corrupt baggage without sounding so altruistic.

This is the unchanging—indeed, unchangeable—face of government, and it is the same today as it has always been. When government assists welfare recipients, labor unions, beekeepers, sheepherders, or domestic clothing manufacturers, to name just a few of our hundreds of special interest groups, it does so by forcefully taking property from its rightful possessors.

So much of what we Americans take for granted as "rights" is nothing more than the property of our neighbors, given to us by a government that knows human weakness will always crave free property and guaranteed welfare. There exists no right to

Medicaid, Medicare, Social Security, welfare, food stamps, health insurance, college education, housing, rent control, farm subsidies, or any other form of aid that the government may next decide to distribute.

I find it fascinating that government today spends the greatest part of its time and energy doing ***precisely and exactly*** what it was hired to prevent others from doing to us.

CHAPTER EIGHT

Federalism and Other Checks and Balances

"CERTAIN ENUMERATED OBJECTS"[191]

When our old friend the Enumeration listed federal powers and left almost all unnamed powers to the states, federalism, a dual government scheme, was born.

A great deal has been written about the blessings and benefits of federalism. You've probably heard the "laboratories of democracy" angle, a great benefit indeed, but there is much more. There are even wartime advantages—when the Brits, for example, delivered the traditional death blow to an enemy in war, the burning of our capital in August of 1814, our decentralized power system allowed us to continue fighting without missing a beat.

Still, there are some things about federalism that at first blush seem so outlandish that they cannot possibly be true. Years ago, I had a conversation with a man who was apoplectic, blind with fury, about a case wherein two children had been raped and murdered. His anger came from the fact that the federal government could not charge the defendant because of the plain and simple fact that ***murder is not a federal crime***. For him, "federal" meant "serious," and Florida's electric chair somehow lacked the gravitas that he sought. I must admit here that the first time I remember hearing about some depraved, murderous beast who could not be charged by the feds, I too was surprised—stunned, actually. Again, at first blush, that just did not seem right.

But, remember the Enumeration. Nowhere in that list is the federal government tasked with crime control. In this chapter, we'll see why that's the case.

Another "strange" thing about federalism—can it really be true that the mere existence of, say, the Department of Education is unconstitutional, or is that just right-wing lunacy? Nope. The DOE is unconstitutional, and again, we'll see why. I hope that, after you read this chapter, you'll agree with me that the only lunacy lies in the fact that the DOE was ever created in the first place. That's a recurring theme with this work—many constitutional truths at first seem shocking, but on second thought are shockingly, obviously good.

Our focus on federalism will be on what I believe are two often overlooked perspectives:

- The compelling logic of a federal system in a nation as diverse as this one has always been, and
- The wondrous way that federalism, when we had a functioning constitution, prevented your money from being stolen from you and delivered to others thousands of miles from you to enrich their lives or to pay for something of absolutely no benefit to you and that you may even abhor with all your soul.

But first, logic. The people of, say, Indiana, are entirely and perfectly capable of self-government. Over the years, they've elected thousands of representatives to a multitude of offices. They have a bicameral legislature, a governor, and a 200+ year history of sane, rational, peaceful self-governance.

The people of Indiana are supremely qualified to determine ***all*** their laws concerning crime, education, zoning, driving age, drinking age, marriage age, salaries and terms of state officials, and on and on and on and on. The list of things the people of Indiana are capable of doing without federal assistance, funding, or input would fill a tome so huge as to put a Gutenberg Bible to shame.

The people of the state of Indiana ***cannot***, however, defend California from foreign invasion, treat with France on behalf of the other states, or settle a water dispute between North and South Carolina.

Does anything more need to be said of federalism?

How about...who is better equipped to handle the crime problems of the city of Billings, Montana—the citizens, police, and elected officials of Billings, or the federal government in Washington, DC? There are 535 representatives in the Congress; exactly four of them represent Montana. When DC passes unconstitutional crime legislation, how much attention do you suppose the crime problems of Billings receive?

Or...where are the interests of individuals and communities more likely to be recognized, known, or acted upon, city hall or Capitol Hill?

Or...they say you can't fight city hall, but what are your chances of fighting, influencing, or escaping the legislative reach of the federal government?

Federalism allows the people of Texas to live with a government of their liking, while allowing the people of Massachusetts to live with a very different government of their own liking. Interference from the federal government does nothing but disrupt and distort those arrangements.

We could go on and on forever in this vein, but the point is clear—there is no reason whatever to believe even for an instant that the federal government is better equipped to handle the day-to-day legislative issues than city, state, or local bodies.

The federal government does not represent the wishes and desires of the people of ***any*** state, county, city, or locality better than the governments on those levels. How could it? After all, the federal government is as different and distinct from the governments of the various states as the governments of small towns are different and distinct from their state governments. So why would one have the federal government meddling in New York's affairs any more than one would have the government in Albany determining the exact placement of Yield signs in the town of Rome, New York?

Here, in the practical nature of federalism, we have yet one more of those stunningly simple, brutally obvious, undeniable truths that is instantly grasped and realized the moment one is exposed to it. Yet this concept, like so many others that are integral to our Constitution, is nothing short of foreign, alien, and unheard of to most Americans. Again, I've never met a soul who pointed out, for example, that the 1994 crime bill (back in the news in 2020 because Biden was getting heat for having supported it) was unconstitutional because crime control is not listed in the Enumeration.

Crime, by the way, is a good way to understand federalism. Is crime control not a federal responsibility because it is unimportant? Absolutely not. Crime control is clearly, obviously, and vitally important. The federal/not federal issue comes down to who is best positioned to handle a problem, not how important the problem is.

Some defend federal intervention in crime control and other areas traditionally thought of as state concerns by asking, "What could possibly be wrong with the federal government deciding to spend a certain amount of its money in all the states on our crime problems, or any other good cause? After all, federal spending on crime does not prevent the people of Billings from enacting their own measures on top of the federal ones."

I am always amazed at how many intelligent, educated people (even elected officials who should certainly know better) think along these lines. The great flaw of course is that the federal government ***has no money of its own to so generously give away***. Almost every single dime the federal government spreads around the states comes from the states in the first place.

Speaking of dimes, if only I had one every time some nitwit said, "Well, if the state of Idaho doesn't want to give in to the feds on the fifty-five miles per hour speed limit, then they can also give up those federal highway dollars!"

So where did those "federal" dollars come from again?

This illustrates yet another serious flaw in federal government intervention into areas where it has no business. We'll stick with the 1994 crime bill as a handy proxy for unconstitutional federal spending.

The federal government, through the crime bill, in essence said to the states, "Okay, I'm gonna take $10 from each and every one of you. I am then gonna give it back to you, after subtracting my overhead, on the condition that you spend it in a manner of my choosing."

Now, this bizarre and ludicrous arrangement would be bad enough if the states all contributed to the federal kitty in proportionate amounts, but such is not the case. For every dollar the federal government collects, some states give more, and they give more year after year after year, while other states ***get*** more. While states can and do move around a bit on the list, it remains a fact that the citizens of Virginia, North Dakota, Kansas, and Hawaii are consistently forced against their will to send their tax dollars to states such as Mississippi and Alabama. How is this defensible?

We are not talking about pennies from heaven here to be spent on crime policy where nothing was to be spent before. This is the federal government telling the states what they will do with their limited resources. Where is the logic there? Does this shuffling around of resources sound efficient? What makes this right?

Presume even that State X wanted to spend the exact amount on crime prevention that the crime bill dictated. Surely, then, it would be they who should decide on ***what*** to spend the funds, be it midnight basketball, riot guns, or counseling for at-risk youth. Where is the sense in taking money from Maryland, letting representatives from 49 other states play around with it, only to hand back some of it with federal strings attached?

Let's take it one step further. State X, by some miracle, desired not only to spend to the exact penny what the feds had in mind, they also were going to spend it on exactly and precisely what the feds desired. So again: why take $10 from them, minus overhead, just to hand it back to them so that they could do what they were going to do all along?

Some would say that certain poor states need the extra money that they receive from federal programs. We need not refer to the

Framers to gauge the justness of such a welfare scheme; we need only point out that the state of Montana has a perfectly functioning, legitimate, representative government. She has a number of both state and federal representatives. Now we must ask ourselves this question: Would the duly elected government of the state of Montana ***ever*** tax its citizens in order to pay for goods and services to be delivered to West Virginia? Can anyone seriously contend that this would happen?

Now what kind of legitimate government takes money from its citizens in direct contradiction of their wishes and the wishes of all of its elected officials and sends it hundreds or even thousands of miles away to be enjoyed by the citizens of another state?

Beyond the logic of the thing, federalism represents yet another significant minority protection simply because the concept recognizes the undeniable truth that different people living in different circumstances, and in different parts of the country, have vastly different interests, ideas, mores, and ways of thinking about public policy.

Under the federal system, the citizens of even the smallest state were perfectly secure in their right to self-determination and were able to preserve their customs, their institutions, their culture, their self-rule, and their very way of life. Specifically, and sticking with our crime theme, under a federal system, the people of Texas could focus on, say, punishing criminals, while the people of Massachusetts would be entirely free to take a wholly different and thoroughly liberal approach of rehabilitation and counseling. Under a federal system, where the people of the individual states, instead of the citizens of the entire United States, dictate policy, towns and communities, and even entire regions are secure from the tyranny of the majority. The Framers knew that without a federal form of government, the more populous states or more powerful regions would ride roughshod over the rights of their weaker neighbors.

Over half of the federally elected representatives from eight different states (Louisiana, Minnesota, Missouri, Oklahoma, Oregon, Texas, Virginia, and West Virginia) voted against the crime bill. Why do the citizens of New York get to tell the citizens of Oregon how to spend their money or how to handle their criminals? Did senators sitting in Washington, DC, know that the citizens of Texas and Oklahoma really wanted this legislation and that their representatives were out of touch with them? Was the federal government in possession of some obscure bits of information, endowing them with a greater insight into Missouri's crime problems than the citizens of Missouri? Is there something about the federal government in general that renders the knowledge and abilities of its officials superior to those of local officials? Why was the federal government empowered to take the property of the citizens of West Virginia in order to force upon them a law against their wishes on a matter of purely local concern?

The federal system our Framers gave us was designed to protect the citizens of those eight states. If every single living, breathing soul on this planet, excepting the citizens of Minnesota, desired that the crime bill be passed, the Constitution still came down on the side of those in Minnesota who did not.

There is something about all this that instantly strikes one as thoroughly just and right. If the people and the elected representatives of those eight states are not to decide how best to handle their own crime problems, ***then who is***?

We must keep in mind that the problem here is ***not*** that some states do not always get their way. Of course they don't. If, for example, the federal government located a new army base in Arkansas to the chagrin of the people of California, then the Californians would not have much to complain about. The federal government is properly charged with the national defense, and it would be impossible, and indeed ridiculous, for it to try to please every state with every one of its actions. But we are talking here of areas and issues that the federal government simply has no business meddling in, neither constitutionally, nor logically, nor morally.

For readers who still have a difficult time accepting that the federal government was intended to have no role (outside of certain, very specific issues like piracy, jurisdiction on federal property, etc.) in such a vital government concern like crime control, or that its duties were sharply defined and limited to certain enumerated items, it is most helpful, vital even, to have some familiarity with the context in which the federal government came into existence. Knowing the context of this story brings us extremely close to knowing ***all*** we need to know.

At the time of the Constitutional Convention, the people and their states enjoyed great freedom. They were, in essence, 13 separate countries, and they paid no taxes to the central government except on a voluntary basis. The government proposed in

Philadelphia was openly and admittedly far more powerful than was the one it would replace. This naturally gave rise, among the people and the states, to fears of tyranny from this new federal authority. They feared it would be too powerful, too distant, and too remote, and that it would mark a return to the exact same situation they had overthrown in the Revolution. This question of the proposed jurisdiction of the federal government was ***the*** issue during the ratification process.

Again, that is why, lacking the Enumeration/federalism that defined and curtailed federal power, the Bill of Rights ***would*** have been far and away the most important part of the Constitution—saying what is off-limits to the federal government is infinitely more important than saying the feds may establish a post office.

Every debate, every concern, every contested clause of the Constitution came back to this one overriding issue of what the federal government could or could not do.

Following the Convention, the Framers spent many months promising the people that the new government would not be too powerful, would respect its limits, and would govern over only those matters where the Constitution clearly gave it authority. Three of the Framers wrote five hundred pages of promises known as *The Federalist Papers*, promises that the federal government would have only so much power and no more. Promises that the states and the people would remain largely sovereign. Five hundred pages of promises, and virtually each one was a rebuttal to a charge that the federal government would not respect its bounds, or that even if it did, its proposed powers were too broad in any event.

To know this story, to know this context, enables the modern reader to easily cut through the fog of obfuscation whenever a debate on the constitutionality of one measure or another arises. Knowing this story transforms what was at first an unthinkable statement about the federal government lacking jurisdiction to pass a crime bill into a logical, easily defensible position. Would the states, having absolute and total control over their own criminal law policies, have voluntarily decided to share that power with representatives and senators from other states? Would they have voluntarily bundled up a bunch of cash and sent it to New York with instructions to let legislators from other states pick over it and then send some of the cash back with legally binding dictates on how to handle the miscreants within their borders? ***This*** idea, not a lack of federal jurisdiction, is what is truly unthinkable.

Now let's see what the Framers had to say about federalism/the Enumeration/limited federal powers.

> *In the first place, it is to be remembered, that the general government is not to be charged with the whole power of making and administering laws: its jurisdiction is limited to certain* ***enumerated*** *objects, which concern all the members of the republic, but which are not to be attained by the separate provisions of any.*
>
> — James Madison[192]

An entire consolidation of the states into one complete national sovereignty, would imply an entire subordination of the parts; and whatever powers might remain in them, would be altogether dependent on the general will. But as the plan of the convention aims only at a partial union or consolidation, the state governments would clearly retain all the rights of sovereignty which they before had, and which were not, by that act, exclusively delegated to the United States.

— Alexander Hamilton[193]

In this relation, then, the proposed government cannot be deemed a national one; since its jurisdiction extends to certain enumerated objects only, and leaves to the several states, a residuary and inviolable sovereignty over all other objects.

— James Madison[194]

Do these principles, in fine, require that the powers of the general government should be limited, and that, beyond this limit, the states should be left in possession of their sovereignty and independence? We have seen that in the new government, as in the old, the general powers are limited; and that the states, in all unenumerated cases, are left in the enjoyment of their sovereign and independent jurisdiction.

— James Madison[195]

The powers delegated by the proposed constitution to the federal government, are few and defined. Those which are to remain in the state governments, are numerous and indefinite. The former will be exercised principally on external objects, as war, peace, negotiation, and foreign commerce; with which last the power of taxation will, for the most part, be connected. The powers reserved to the several states will extend to all the objects which, in the ordinary course of affairs, concern the lives, liberties, and properties of the people; and the internal order, improvement, and prosperity of the state.

The operations of the federal government will be most extensive and important in times of war and danger; those of the state governments in times of peace and security.

— James Madison[196]

The famous Supreme Court decision *Marbury v. Madison*, though it dealt with other issues, rested finally on this exact same recognition of the federal legislature's constitutionally limited powers.

The powers of the legislature are defined, and limited; and that those limits may not be mistaken, or forgotten, the constitution is written. To what purpose are powers limited, and to what purpose is that limitation committed to writing, if these limits may, at any time, be passed by those intended to be restrained?

— John Marshall[197]

"The powers of the legislature are defined, and limited..." God, what a dream that would be. Nowadays those defined limits include spending $7.9 million to promote journalism in Sri Lanka, including ensuring journalists use "gender sensitive" language. But don't worry—contrary to earlier reports, it seems that while your money was sent to Sri Lanka for journalistic purposes, only ***some*** of it was gender-sensitivity related. Well! That leaves me numb with relief. How about you?

Our government treats us like high-producing trained apes, and there is no end in sight.

CHAPTER NINE

The Bill of Very Few Rights Strikes Again

"THOSE LIMITS MAY NOT BE MISTAKEN OR FORGOTTEN"[198]

LET US REVISIT our old friend, the Constitution-murdering Bill of Very Few Rights. We will examine some contradictory quotations illustrating the nearly impossible-to-believe power of the Bill to create confusion in the human mind, and destroy the Constitution in the process.

The first five quotations demonstrate a thorough knowledge of the limits placed on the federal government by the Constitution. They come from a hugely successful book that spent four months on *The New York Times* Best Seller list. The author—we'll call him Bert—is identified on his Wikipedia page as a federal judge, solicitor general of the United States, and Yale Law School professor. Clearly we have here a man with as fine and deep an understanding of our Constitution and its principles as we could ever wish (except, perhaps, for my own fine and deep constitutional understanding).

> There is little doubt that those who framed and ratified the Constitution ***enumerated*** the powers given the national legislature—and for good measure added the tenth amendment...so that the federal government could not govern many aspects of life.[199]

Bert is wrong with that nonsense about "those who framed and ratified the Constitution" adding the Tenth Amendment, but he's 100% correct about the important part—the Enumeration, the original and better bill of rights, being written to limit federal power.

> That freedom [to leave a state whose laws one finds onerous] would be drastically curtailed if the national government had the power to impose all of the same burdens [as a state government].[200]

Bert again refers to the Enumeration above. The only thing keeping the feds from imposing the same burdens as the states is the Enumeration. It's certainly not the Bill of Very Few Rights, which would, as it is misunderstood, leave to the feds the power to set, for example, the age for legal marriage.

> In this sense, federalism[201] is the constitutional guarantee most protective of the individual's freedom to make his own choices. There is much to be said, therefore, for a

> Court that attempted to preserve federalism, which is a real constitutional principle, by setting limits to national powers.[202]
>
> The Constitution does indicate that there are defined national powers and that they have limits. The fact that the powers of Congress are enumerated in article I, section 8, demonstrates that Congress was not intended to have unlimited powers, even aside from the specific limitations stated, primarily, in the Bill of Rights. That necessary inference is reinforced by the tenth amendment.[203]

Our hero also approvingly quotes Justice Marshall's previously cited words from *Marbury v. Madison* on the "defined and limited" federal powers.[204]

Let me interpret every one of the above-quoted words for you—the federal government's powers are confined to those laid out in the Enumeration. Thus, the federal government may not tell you how to worship, tell you that you cannot buy a home, or tell you which chickens to buy. Simple.

Now, in our second set of passages, we have another *NY Times* best-selling author (we'll call him Rob). This author's knowledge of the Constitution is poor indeed, even though he was once a judge on the U.S. Court of Appeals for the D.C. Circuit and a nominee for the U.S. Supreme Court. As you will see, Rob is a big fan of the Bill of Rights and is entirely ignorant of the Enumeration. This leads him, inevitably and invariably, to the conclusion that we have no rights in this world outside of those sad few listed in the Bill of Very Few Rights.

> The only thing majorities may not do is invade the liberties the Constitution ***specifies.***[205]

Talk about sugarcoating! What Rob meant to say was "All federal law is legitimate, except the ones that invade the liberties specified in the Bill of Rights."

If I recall, there was a reason the Framers didn't want a bill of rights. Oh, yes! I remember now. It was because a bill of rights would make people think that "The only thing majorities may not do is invade the liberties the Constitution specifies."

And Rob thinks saying "majorities" makes it sound legitimate. That's a point we discussed earlier—even if the feds actually did poll the majority before stealing your money, would it be legitimate? And do you think the feds really checked to see if the majority wanted to spend $7.9 million to teach Sri Lankan journalists how to avoid binary gendered language?

Trust me, dear reader, you have the right to get married free of federal government interference, even though said right is not listed in the Bill of Very Few Rights. The Enumeration fixed that for us.

Rob continues,

> We govern ourselves democratically, except on those occasions, ***few in number*** though crucially important,

> when the Constitution places a topic beyond the reach of majorities.[206]

"Few in number..." Yes, of course it's few in number, because Rob is referring to the disastrous Bill of Very Few Rights. Look at that passage. More sugarcoating. Again, "we govern ourselves democratically" translates to "The feds may tell us what to do."

Next, Rob criticizes a man who wants judges to protect liberties not mentioned in the Constitution. Rob wants judges to protect "***only*** those liberties ***actually mentioned*** in the Constitution."[207] In other words, the Bill of Rights. The Enumeration is unknown to this federal "judge."

Rob then takes Justice Taney to task for the Dred Scott decision. I'll take Rob's word for it (though as you have seen, taking his word for anything is a dicey proposition) that Justice Taney found that "there can be no valid federal law against slaveholding anywhere in the United States."[208]

> How did Taney know that slave ownership was a constitutional right? Such a right is nowhere to be found in the Constitution.[209]

Later, he writes,

> It is clear that Congress had the power to outlaw racially restrictive covenants [among wholly private parties].[210]

Rob also cites approvingly the opinions of one sitting justice and three former justices who have no qualms with the feds banning flag burning.

All of the above can mean only two things: Rob is entirely ignorant of the Enumeration and knows only the Bill of Very Few Rights. Okay, it means three things: those first two, plus Rob is a terrible judge.

I guess it also means that the federal government's powers are limited only by the Bill of Rights. Thus, the federal government may tell you that you cannot buy a home, wear eye shadow, or marry whom you choose. Such rights are not, after all, found in the Bill of Rights. Simple.

The problem with ***all*** these quotations, the good ones and the bad ones, in case you've not guessed, is that they are all ***from the same man writing the same book***, Justice Robert Bork, in *The Tempting of America*.

Think about that for a moment. ***All of the above quotations are from the same man writing in the same book!***

How can this possibly be? Bork holds the absolutely diametrically opposed views that the federal government is limited in its power and defined in its jurisdiction, yet, amazingly, can at the same time legislate on any topic whatsoever not specifically prohibited by the Bill of Rights. In direct and absolute contradiction to the first citations, Bork believes that we have only those liberties actually listed in the Bill of Rights. Again, this is despite his clear and specific words to the contrary, and this is despite his understanding of enumerated powers, where they are located, and how they work. Just take a moment to marvel at what the mere existence of the Bill of Rights can do to a person's thinking!

Remember Bork's own words: "those who framed and ratified the Constitution ***enumerated*** the powers given the national legislature."[211] Very good. So where lies the federal authority to regulate private covenants, ban flag burning, or abolish slavery? Where? Point to it. Show me that enumerated power.

I do wish, by the way, that Bork had picked an example other than the Dred Scott case. Who, after all, wants to attack an argument, any argument, that finds a legislative power to end slavery?

I cannot tell you how much I wish that the words "slave" and "slavery" were meaningless gibberish, words nobody had ever heard, because in all the entire history of the world, there had never once been a thing called a slave, or a thing called slavery. Slavery is a bad, evil, corrupt, and irredeemable thing, and it pains me greatly that it has so permanently stained the nation that I love. But my wishes are irrelevant because slavery has indeed put its filthy mark on my nation and on our Constitution. Sadly, the federal government was not (short of a constitutional amendment) empowered to abolish or regulate slavery.[212] The fact isn't just sad, however. It is also one of the most unassailable and highly documented facts in all of American history.

Remember, we noted earlier that ***the*** issue at the Convention, the colossus that towered above all others, was the question of what the federal government was empowered to do and what it was prohibited from doing. Somehow, a man of Bork's huge stature and education entirely missed the fact that at the Convention, the southern states were constantly threatening to bolt the proceedings if slavery were threatened. If the general issue of federal jurisdiction was the biggest of all, then slavery was one of the biggest subset questions of that issue. It was the rotting, stinking carcass, lurking in a corner, simultaneously affecting and polluting the entire affair.

And the fact remains—the southern states were never going to sign on to a government that could, 10 minutes after ratification, abolish slavery. Period. I literally stopped going to school after the sixth grade, and I've known this for almost my entire life. How does Bork not know it? I blame the Bill of Very Few Rights.

The distressing nature of slavery does not in any way affect the absolute simplicity of the legal question at hand, and it doesn't change the fact that Bork is dead wrong. If the federal government had the legal power to end slavery, where, exactly, is that power found in the Constitution? Certainly not in the Enumeration, which Bork himself identifies as the place where federal jurisdiction is defined.

No, that power can only come from the nonsensical belief that the owning of slaves was not specifically singled out in the Bill of Rights, and therefore, like the right to have children, it does not exist.

Bork's confusion goes even deeper, however. Look at how he contradicts himself not only in a single book, but ***even in a single paragraph.***

> The tenth amendment is clearly a guarantee of federalism. It confirms that federal powers were ***intended to be limited*** [by the Enumeration, which gives to the people freedom from federal power that is almost ***limitless***] and that the powers not lodged in the national government remained with the states, if the states had such powers under their own constitutions, and, if not, the powers were still held by the people. The ninth amendment appears to serve a parallel function by guaranteeing that the rights of the people specified already in state constitutions were not cast in doubt by the fact that only a ***limited set of rights*** was guaranteed by the federal charter [in the Bill of Rights].[213]

Federal power was limited by the Enumeration, but only a limited set of rights was guaranteed by the Constitution in the Bill of Rights? Ridiculous.

CHAPTER TEN

Justifying the Leviathan

"A POWER TO DESTROY"[214]

ATTACKS ON THE notion that the Constitution significantly constrains federal government jurisdiction these days usually focus on the "general welfare"[215] and "necessary and proper"[216] clauses. These clauses, say the ignorant and those who know better but are desperate to expand federal authority, are said to empower the federal government to do damn near anything it wants, at any time it wants, for any reason it wants.

This is an extraordinary claim, even an unbelievable one, given that the men who wrote the Constitution were confronted with that exact accusation and responded quite forcefully and convincingly that these clauses absolutely did not confer any grant of power to the government.

They even said so in *The Federalist Papers*, which was not, as noted earlier, an obscure body of work, making it mind-boggling that people, especially federal authorities of all stripes, elected or otherwise, can actually get away with claiming such a grant exists. Before reading the Framers' words on these clauses, however, we might just want to point out that logical reasoning alone can deflate the idea that these clauses are as powerful as some might have us believe.

First, recall once more the context in which the Constitution was ratified. Again, we ask the question: Would the people ever have ratified a document that gave virtually unlimited power to a distant federal government after having just fought a war to rid themselves of such a government? It seems unlikely. Would the Framers have even thought to create such a government? Did they possess some secret, heretofore undiscovered desire for an all-powerful central government?

Second, because such a broad reading of these clauses would indeed establish a government almost unlimited in power, what could possibly be the reason for the rest of the Constitution? Why write a 4,600-word constitution, just to insert a clause at about one-third of the way in, that says, essentially, "This government is to have unlimited powers. You may thus ignore every word that has come before and every word that shall follow this clause."? Why did the Framers spend a long, arduous summer locked in secret debate simply to write a document that could be summed up in a few paragraphs? What could possibly be the purpose of all these checks and balances we've discussed if government was to be unlimited in scope, power, and jurisdiction?

Enough theorizing; let us see what the Framers had to say.

> *With respect to the words "general welfare," I have always regarded them as qualified by the detail of powers connected with them.*[217] *To take them in a literal and unlimited sense would be a metamorphosis of the Constitution into a character which there is a host of proofs was not contemplated by its creators.*
>
> — James Madison[218]

> *If Congress can do whatever in their discretion can be done by money, and will promote the General Welfare, the Government is no longer a limited one.*
>
> — James Madison[219]

Thomas Jefferson's view was the same, saying Congress does not have "unlimited powers to provide for the general welfare, but were restrained to those specifically enumerated."[220]

In *Federalist* 41, yet another promise to the people that the federal government was to be limited, Madison again makes the case against the totalitarian reading of the general welfare clause. Madison answers the critics who fear that the general welfare clause "amounts to an unlimited commission to exercise every power, which may be alleged to be necessary for the common defense or general welfare,"[221] critics who fear, in short, that the clause will be precisely what so many people today want it to be.

> Had no other enumeration or definition of the powers of the congress been found in the constitution, than the general expressions just cited, the authors of the objection might have had some colour for it; though it would have been difficult to find a reason for so awkward a form of describing an authority to legislate in all possible cases. A power to destroy the freedom of the press, the trial by jury, or even to regulate the course of descents, or the forms of conveyances, must be very singularly expressed by the terms "to raise money for the general welfare."
>
> But what colour can the objection have, when a specification [the enumeration again] of the objects alluded to by these general terms, immediately follows; and is not even separated by a longer pause than a semicolon? If the different parts of the same instrument ought to be so expounded, as to give meaning to every part which will bear it, shall one part of the same sentence be excluded altogether from a share in the meaning; and shall the more doubtful and indefinite terms be retained in their full extent, and the clear and precise expressions be denied any signification whatsoever? For what purpose could the enumeration of particular powers be inserted, if these and all others were meant to be included in the preceding general power? Nothing is more natural nor common, than first to use a general phrase, and then to explain and qualify it by a recital of particulars. But the idea of an

> enumeration of particulars, which neither explain nor qualify the general meaning, and can have no other effect than to confound and mislead, is an absurdity which, as we are reduced to the dilemma of charging either on the authors of the objection, or on the authors of the constitution, we must take the liberty of supposing, had not its origin with the latter.[222]

In *Federalist* 33, we find much the same thing on the necessary and proper clause. Again, we see the promise repeated: the federal government is to be limited in scope and to have jurisdiction over only those things found in the Enumeration.

> *These two clauses [the other clause he speaks of is the supremacy clause] have been the sources of much virulent invective, and petulant declamation, against the proposed constitution. They have been held up to the people in all the exaggerated colours of misrepresentation; as the pernicious engines by which their local governments were to be destroyed, and their liberties exterminated; as the hideous monster whose devouring jaws would spare neither sex nor age, nor high nor low, nor sacred nor profane; and yet, strange as it may appear, after all this clamour, to those who may not have happened to contemplate them in the same light, it may be affirmed with perfect confidence, that the constitutional operation of the intended government would be precisely the same, if these clauses were entirely obliterated, as if they were repeated in every article. They are only declaratory of a truth which would have resulted by necessary and unavoidable*

implication from the very act of constituting a federal government, and vesting it with certain specified powers. This is so clear a proposition, that moderation itself can scarcely listen to the railings which have been so copiously vented against this part of the plan, without emotions that disturb its equanimity.

What is a power, but the ability or faculty of doing a thing? What is the ability to do a thing, but the power of employing the means necessary to its execution? What is a LEGISLATIVE *power, but a power of making* LAWS*? What are the means to execute a* LEGISLATIVE *power, but* LAWS*? What is the power of laying and collecting taxes, but a legislative power, or a power of making laws, to lay and collect taxes? What are the proper means of executing such a power, but necessary and proper laws?*

This simple train of inquiry furnishes us at once with a test of the true nature of the clause complained of. It conducts us to this palpable truth, that a power to lay and collect taxes, must be a power to pass all laws necessary and proper for the execution of that power: and what does the unfortunate and calumniated provision in question do, more than declare the same truth; to wit, that the national legislature, to whom the power of laying and collecting taxes had been previously given, might, in the execution of that power, pass all laws necessary and proper to carry it into effect? I have applied these observations thus particularly to the power of taxation; because it is the immediate subject under consideration, and because it is the most important of the authorities proposed to be conferred upon the union. But the same process will lead to the same result, in relation to all other powers declared in the constitution. And it is expressly to execute these powers that the sweeping clause, as it has been affectedly called, authorizes the national legislature to pass all necessary and proper laws. If there is any thing exceptionable, it must be sought for in the specific powers, upon which this general declaration is predicated. The declaration itself, though it may be chargeable with tautology or redundancy, is at least perfectly harmless.

— Alexander Hamilton[223]

CHAPTER ELEVEN

Conclusion

"ERRORS AND DELUSIONS"[224]

THE CONSTITUTION IS dead. Long dead, actually. With the passing of the Enumeration, the federal government has almost no limits, and your cash can be seized in any sum for any reason at any time.

Yes, we still have scheduled elections and a three-branch government, but the Enumeration, far and away the most vital constitutional mechanism to limit the power of the government and protect the liberties of the people, simply does not exist in any meaningful way at all.

But how did we lose the Constitution in the first place? Who's to blame?

Politicians, of course, come in for a great deal of blame. Few things on Earth are as reliable, after all, as the politician who trades the property of one for the votes of two. And then there is a near-endless string of breathtakingly corrupt Supreme Court decisions that led to at least half a century of unchecked expansion of federal power. Ten billion words would not be enough to adequately write even the first chapter of that book...

And human nature, of course, showed its ugly and common side; the lust for the property of others, it seems, is never sated, never quenched. One can even debate whether the Framers were quite up to the task, whether their checks and balances were strong enough, but the system worked remarkably well for about 140 years, and could any collection of humans possibly have done better?

Others blame the astonishingly rapid decline of our freedom (a.k.a. the astonishingly rapid growth of the federal government) on the Great Depression and world wars, or the shrinking of the continent by radio, television, planes, trains, and automobiles, but in the end, I feel it must always come back to human nature, back to the people.

I speak not of the greed of the hundreds upon hundreds of separate tiny minorities who each took a small bite of the pie, until there were so many taking as to be a majority. No. I speak of the majority who, somewhere along the line, fell asleep (more like slipped into a coma) at the switch. In the end, the most perfect Constitution imaginable, even one designed by the Creator himself, would amount to a mere parchment barrier if almost nobody cared. And that seems to be what has happened in this country. It is an undeniable fact that if the citizens of this nation truly cared, property would again be safe. But maybe this isn't fair. Maybe property was doomed, not because the people stopped paying attention, but because the Constitution ceased being an antimajoritarian document after being amended to allow for the direct election of both the president and Senate.

With the direct election of the entirety of the legislative branch and the president, and with the discarding of the Enumeration, we now have something very close to direct democracy. Should we be even remotely surprised at the state of our property then? The Framers certainly wouldn't be. Still, others would point out that the system was certainly antimajoritarian at the time the Constitution was legally transformed into a majoritarian charter. In other words, the Constitution's safeguards weren't strong enough to preserve its vital antimajoritarian nature.

So, while it may be impossible to accurately place the blame for this sorry state of affairs, the fact remains that if the people, the majority, can be instilled with some sense of respect for their own property and the property of others, then all may not be irretrievably lost.

The most obvious way to bring this about is through education. School-age children seem to take to the philosophy of freedom and self-autonomy rather easily, at least as it relates to permitting bizarre and deviant behavior. It shouldn't be too difficult to make our children realize that the doctrine of tolerance means not only that they have the freedom to smoke dope and worship Satan, sport iridescent blue mohawks, shun bathing, and pierce their bodies with enough metal to ballast oil freighters, but that they have the right to dispense the fruits of their own labor as they see fit.

But then again, this might be asking a bit much. The ***government*** has a virtual monopoly on our education system, making one wonder just how likely it is that that same government would teach children the Framers' thoughts on money, government, and freedom.

Barring formal education, then, we could, just to be radical for a moment, stop dismissing the words of the Framers as out of date and actually pay attention to what they said. Here, for example, is an all-too-typical passage from a college textbook, remarking on some of the choice words the Founders had on the subject of mankind.

> Certainly, the anti-democratic sentiments expressed by many of the Founding Fathers strike the modern student of government as unenlightened. Perhaps they were. It must be remembered, however, that they were sailing on uncharted seas. They were not familiar with universal suffrage and mass democracy. Nor were many of their countrymen prepared for the duties that accompany political liberty.[225]

The Founders were unfamiliar with mass democracy? I can't agree with this. The Founders studied the dysfunctional horrors of ancient democracy and were experiencing its chaos in their own lives. They were sickened by democracy, producing, predictably, the nightmare of legal theft through the creation of paper money.

The implication of that quotation is clear and unmistakable—the Founders had something to say for their time and place, but today we have moved on and we are far better prepared for self-government than were the people way back then.

Here is a perfect example of simply not taking the Framers/Founders seriously. The Framers' thoughts and words centered on man's immutable ***nature***—not a thing that changes in a few hundred years or is effected by a college degree or a fat paycheck. Man has not changed. Our wealth and education have not elevated us to the point where we can be trusted with government power. The evidence for that is overwhelming and undeniable. The Framers feared that men would use political power to take the property of other men. How could anybody observe today's all-too-democratic system and not see that they were correct?

While I am not one to look back on the good old days, finding great wisdom in the homespun philosophies of uneducated rustics, it still seems to me undeniable that the citizens of the Revolutionary era were far, far ***better*** equipped for self-government than we are today.

First, they actually knew what property was and didn't believe everything they owned was legitimately up for grabs to any politician anywhere at any time. Today, not one in one hundred Americans realizes that possession of his paycheck is a right of any kind whatsoever, let alone that it is the most important right, and that most federal spending is morally outrageous as opposed to being merely annoying or even a positive blessing.

In Revolutionary America, government plans to tax for the "social good" would have been met with bullets, not wonderment at why the government didn't just go ahead and solve ***all*** the world's problems as opposed to only that poverty thing. Those uneducated citizens paid zero dollars to the federal government for welfare programs, and for every dollar they did send to Washington, we send ***2,130***.

They went to war with history's mightiest nation over the principle involved in a few nearly insignificant taxes. We work three-and-a-half months a year to feed government's insatiable lust for property, and roughly half of us think even that is not enough. We political sophisticates of today go around numbly mouthing nonsense about dying for the right to be rude and bizarre, while working like trained apes to fill the coffers of and feed the self-love of career politicians.

Furthermore, the citizen of Revolutionary America was a tad bit more mature than we are today. Let us look back to *Federalist* 63 to see just one example of this.

> To a people as little blinded by prejudice, or corrupted by flattery, as those whom I address, I shall not scruple to add, that such an institution [the Senate] may be sometimes necessary as a defense to the people against their own temporary errors and delusions.[226]

Here is James Madison telling his fellow citizens that they need a Senate somewhat removed from their control to ensure their happiness. Again, this blunt and unflattering language is just one of many examples contained in *The Federalist Papers*, which were published in newspapers throughout the nation for public consumption. Can you begin to imagine the public foot-stomping, the infantile temper tantrum, the juvenile hissy fit of historic proportion if a high public official were to say something like that today? And remember, not only were Madison and company not required to apologize, resign, and undergo sensitivity training, ***but they actually won their argument.*** They convinced the people to sign on to a government that was far less democratic than the one being replaced. We, it seems, are not quite so "little blinded by prejudice or corrupted by flattery"[227] as the unprepared citizens of yesterday.

Books like this usually end the same way—with a statement to the effect that "It is in our hands, people! Only we the people have the power to change things by sending a powerful message to our rulers in Washington. Let's wake up, America, and take action!" This is largely true. Things are, of course, in our hands, and that is precisely why I hold out so little hope of salvation. With half the population in favor of sending more and more of our freedom to Washington, with millions more of us asleep at the switch, and with millions more actively gorging themselves on the labor of the first two groups, and with decades upon decades of rapidly growing government becoming more powerful by the minute, it is difficult indeed to see much hope for the future.

When we say that things are in "our hands," we are largely speaking of a direct democracy, one without limits in our case, and we know what the Framers had to say about that.

Endnotes

1 The Debates in the Several State Conventions, on the Adoption of the Federal Constitution, as Recommended by the General Convention at Philadelphia, in 1787, 2nd ed., vol. II, ed. Jonathan Elliot (Washington: Printed by and for the Editor, 1836), 409.

2 Alexander Hamilton, "No. 84," in The Federalist: On the New Constitution, Written in the Year 1788, by Mr. Hamilton, Mr. Madison, and Mr. Jay: with an Appendix, Containing the Letters of Pacificus and Helvidius, on the Proclamation of Neutrality of 1793; Also, the Original Articles of Confederation, and the Constitution of the United States, with the Amendments Made Thereto (Washington: Jacob Gideon, 1818), 535.

3 Robert A. Goldwin, From Parchment to Power: How James Madison Used the Bill of Rights to Save the Constitution (The AEI Press, 1997), 76.

4 Christopher Collier and James Lincoln Collier, Decision in Philadelphia: The Constitutional Convention of 1787 (Reader's Digest Press, 1987).

5 John Adams, A Defence of the Constitutions of Government of the United States of America, vol. III (London: William Cobbett, 1794), 217.

6 James Madison, Notes of Debates in the Federal Convention of 1787 (Ohio University Press, 1966), 471.

7 Forrest McDonald, Novus Ordo Seclorum: The Intellectual Origins of the Constitution (University Press of Kansas, 1985), 4.

8 Madison, Papers, Purchased by Order of Congress, vol. II, 753.

9 Elliot, Debates in the Several State Conventions, vol. II, 409.

10 Collier and Collier, Decision in Philadelphia, 249.

11 "Framers" (of the Constitution) and "Founding Fathers" are terms invariably conflated with one another, used interchangeably, or both, even in the above quotation. That is a big mistake that we will try to avoid. "Framers" refers to the 55 men at the Constitutional Convention of 1787. "Founders" refers to the six to eight men (lists differ) whose contributions to the nation's creation generally spanned the time before, during, and after the Convention.

12 Federalist, no. 84 (Alexander Hamilton), 535–36, uppercase letters in original.

13 Goldwin, From Parchment to Power, xii.

14 Goldwin, From Parchment to Power, 76.

15 Debates in the Several State Conventions, vol. II, 409.

16 Debates in the Several State Conventions, vol. II, 424.

17 See A.L.A. Schechter Poultry Corp. v. United States, 295 US 495 (1935).

18 The Debates, Resolutions, and Other Proceedings, in Convention, on the Adoption of the Federal Constitution, as Recommended by the General Convention at Philadelphia, on the 17th of September, 1787: With the Yeas and Nays on the Decision of the Main Question, vol. III, ed. Jonathan Elliot (Washington: Printed by and for the Editor, 1830), 238.

19 Elliot, Debates in the Several State Conventions, vol. II, 409.

20 The Debates and Proceedings in the Congress of the United States; with an Appendix, Containing Important State Papers and Public Documents, and All the Laws of a Public Nature; with a Copious Index, Comprising (with Volume II) the Period from March 3, 1789, to March 3, 1791, Inclusive, vol. I, ed. Joseph Gales (Washington: Gales and Seaton, 1834), 456.

21 Federalist, no. 84 (Alexander Hamilton), 535.

22 As we have seen, this is not quite true. At the time of this writing, Madison was pursuing that House seat that he might not have won if he had continued in opposing a bill of rights.

23 George Tucker, The Life of Thomas Jefferson, Third President of the United States, with Parts of His Correspondence Never Before Published, and Notices of His Opinions on Questions of Civil Government, National Policy, and Constitutional Law, vol. I (Philadelphia: Carey, Lea & Blanchard, 1837), 277.

24 McMaster and Stone, Pennsylvania and the Federal Constitution, 252.

25 John Bach McMaster and Frederick D. Stone, eds., Pennsylvania and the Federal Constitution, 1787–1788 (Lancaster, PA: Historical Society of Pennsylvania, 1888), 272.

26 McMaster and Stone, Pennsylvania and the Federal Constitution, 784.

27 U.S. Const. amend. IX.

28 U.S. Const. amend. IX.

29 U.S. Const. amend. X.

30 James Madison, "No. 45," in The Federalist: On the New Constitution, Written in the Year 1788, by Mr. Hamilton, Mr. Madison, and Mr. Jay: with an Appendix, Containing the Letters of Pacificus and Helvidius, on the Proclamation of Neutrality of 1793; Also, the Original Articles of Confederation, and the Constitution of the United States, with the Amendments Made Thereto (Washington: Jacob Gideon, 1818), 292.

31 Adams, Defence of the Constitutions, vol. III, 217.

32 James Madison, Letters and Other Writings of James Madison, Fourth President of the United States, vol. IV (Philadelphia: J. B. Lippincott & Co., 1865), 478.

33 Paul Larkin, "The Framers' Understanding of 'Property'," The Heritage Foundation, July 6, 2020, https://www.heritage.org/economic-and-property-rights/report/the-framers-understanding-property.

34 Tom DeWeese, "Change the Debate and Take Back Liberty Locally," American Policy Center, December 4, 2024, https://americanpolicy.org/2024/12/04/change-the-debate-and-take-back-liberty-locally/, emphasis added.

35 Adams, Defence of the Constitutions, vol. III, 217, upper-case letters in original.

36 Adams, Defence of the Constitutions, vol. III, 216.

37 John Adams, Discourses on Davila: A Series of Papers on Political History (Boston: Russell and Cutler, 1805), 92.

38 Madison, Letters and Other Writings of James Madison, vol. IV, 478.

39 The Records of the Federal Convention of 1787, vol. I, ed. Max Farrand (Yale University Press, 1911), 147.

40 McDonald, Novus Ordo Seclorum, 4, emphasis added.

41 Demian Brady, "Government Spending in Historical Context," National Taxpayers Union Foundation, April 7, 2022, https://www.ntu.org/foundation/tax-page/government-spending-in-historical-context.

42 James Boswell, The Life of Samuel Johnson (New York: Random House, 1701), 511.

43 Thomas Hobbes, Leviathan (London: Andrew Crooke, 1651).

44 Brady, "Government Spending in Historical Context."

45 "How Much Has the U.S. Government Spent This Year?," Fiscal Data, Treasury.gov, accessed March 5, 2025, https://fiscaldata.treasury.gov/americas-finance-guide/federal-spending/.

46 Brady, "Government Spending in Historical Context."

47 Madison, Letters and Other Writings of James Madison, vol. IV, 478.

48 English philosopher to whom we owe a great deal of our founding political principles. Though he died in 1704, he is probably, outside of Madison, the Constitution's most important influence.

49 John Locke, Two Treatises of Government (London: Awnsham and John Churchill, 1690), 301, emphasis in original.

50 Thomas Jefferson, Notes on the State of Virginia (Philadelphia: R. T. Rawle, 1801), 312.

51 Bowers v. Hardwick, 478 U.S. 186 (1986).

52 Locke, Two Treatises of Government, 305–306.

53 S. G. Tallentyre, The Friends of Voltaire (John Murray, 1906), 198–99.

54 James Madison, "No. 10," in The Federalist: On the New Constitution, Written in the Year 1788, by Mr. Hamilton, Mr. Madison, and Mr. Jay: with an Appendix, Containing the Letters of Pacificus and Helvidius, on the Proclamation of Neutrality of 1793; Also, the Original Articles of Confederation, and the Constitution of the United States, with the Amendments Made Thereto (Washington: Jacob Gideon, 1818), 57.

55 Federalist, no. 10 (James Madison), 57.

56 Federalist, no. 10 (James Madison), 59, emphasis added.

57 Federalist, no. 10 (James Madison), 58.

58 Federalist, no. 10 (James Madison), 59, emphasis added.

59 Federalist, no. 10 (James Madison), 60.

60 Federalist, no. 10 (James Madison), 59–60.

61 Federalist, no. 10 (James Madison), 60.

62 Federalist, no. 10 (James Madison), 63–64.

63 Federalist, no. 10 (James Madison), 65.

64 There is one mention of "speech" in the unamended Constitution, but it references a speech delivered by a representative.

65 Madison, Letters and Other Writings of James Madison, vol. IV, 51.

66 Records of the Federal Convention, vol. I, 302.

67 Locke, Two Treatises of Government, 347.

68 James Otis, The Rights of the British Colonies Asserted and Proved (London: J. Almon, 1764), 106.

69 John Dickinson, The Writings of John Dickinson, vol. I, ed. Paul Leicester Ford (Philadelphia: Historical Society of Pennsylvania, 1895), 202.

70 Virginia Declaration of Rights, art. I.

71 John Adams, A Defence of the Constitutions of Government of the United States of America, vol. I (London: C. Dilly, 1787), 131.

72 James Madison, Debates on the Adoption of the Federal Constitution in the Convention Held at Philadelphia 1787 with a Diary of the Debates of the Congress of the Confederation as Reported by James Madison, vol. V, ed. Jonathan Elliot (New York: Burt Franklin, 1787), 435.

73 The Debates and Proceedings in the Congress of the United States; with an Appendix, Containing Important State Papers and Public Documents, and All the Laws of a Public Nature; with a Copious Index, Comprising the Period from December 2, 1793, to March 3, 1795, Inclusive: Third Congress (Washington: Gales and Seaton, 1849), 170.

74 Franklin Pierce, Message from the President of the United States, Returning to the Senate the Bill Entitled "An Act Making a Grant of Public Lands to the Several States for the Bencfit of Indigent Insane, Persons," with a Statement of the Objections Which Have Required Him to Withhold from It His Approval, S. Doc. 56, 33d Cong., 1st sess. (May 3, 1854), http://www.loc.gov/item/2022698826/.

75 Grover Cleveland, Message from the President of the United States, Returning House Bill No. 10203, with His Objections Thereto, 49th Cong., 2d sess. (February 17, 1887).

76 Federalist, no. 10 (James Madison), 59.

77 James Madison, Notes of Debates in the Federal Convention of 1787 (Ohio University Press, 1966), 135.

78 Madison, Letters and Other Writings of James Madison, vol. IV, 22.

79 "Federal Farmer No. 1," in Pamphlets on the Constitution of the United States, Published During Its Discussion by the People 1787–1788, ed. Paul Leicester Ford (Brooklyn, NY: Burt Franklin, 1888), 283, emphasis added.

80 Collier and Collier, Decision in Philadelphia, 46–47.

81 Adams, Discourses on Davila, 92.

82 Rick Lynch, "Paper Money and the Constitution," The Future of Freedom Foundation, January 1, 2009, https://www.fff.org/explore-freedom/article/paper-money-constitution/.

83 Lynch, "Paper Money and the Constitution," emphasis in original.

84 Lynch, "Paper Money and the Constitution."

85 Lynch, "Paper Money and the Constitution."

86 Madison, Debates on the Adoption of the Federal Constitution, vol. V, 321.

87 Lynch, "Paper Money and the Constitution."

88 Madison's "Vices" (before the Convention), Madison's Notes (during the Convention), and The Federalist Papers (after the Convention)

89 Madison, Notes of Debates in the Federal Convention, 471.

90 Madison, Notes of Debates in the Federal Convention, 471.

91 Madison, Notes of Debates in the Federal Convention, 75.

92 Madison, Notes of Debates in the Federal Convention, 78.

93 Madison, Notes of Debates in the Federal Convention, 86.

94 Madison, Notes of Debates in the Federal Convention, 86.
95 Madison, Notes of Debates in the Federal Convention, 89.
96 Madison, Notes of Debates in the Federal Convention, 135.
97 Madison, Notes of Debates in the Federal Convention, 303.
98 Madison, Notes of Debates in the Federal Convention, 305.
99 Madison, Notes of Debates in the Federal Convention, 315.
100 Madison, Notes of Debates in the Federal Convention, 323.
101 Madison, Notes of Debates in the Federal Convention, 339.
102 Madison, Notes of Debates in the Federal Convention, 429.
103 Madison, Notes of Debates in the Federal Convention, 463.
104 James Madison to George Washington, April 16, 1787, The James Madison Papers at the Library of Congress, Library of Congress, http://www.loc.gov/item/mjm012718/.
105 Lynch, "Paper Money and the Constitution."
106 U.S. Const. amend. I.
107 McDonald, Novus Ordo Seclorum, 42.
108 Lynch, "Paper Money and the Constitution," emphasis added.
109 McDonald, Novus Ordo Seclorum, 288, emphasis added.
110 McDonald, Novus Ordo Seclorum, 288, emphasis added.
111 Encyclopedia Britannica, "sumptuary law," accessed March 7, 2025, https://www.britannica.com/topic/sumptuary-law.
112 Federalist, no. 10 (James Madison), 65.
113 Adams, Discourses on Davila, 92.
114 English journalist who believed in an over reliance on "the people" as the guardians of liberty.
115 Adams, Defence of the Constitutions, vol. III, 216–17, uppercase letters in original.
116 Jonathan Elliot, ed., The Debates in the Several State Conventions, on the Adoption of the Federal Constitution, as Recommended by the General Convention at

Philadelphia in 1787, 2nd ed., vol. III (Washington: Printed by and for the Editor, 1856), 355.

117 And how they get around the last 14 words of the Second Amendment is a question best left to mental health experts.

118 U.S. Const. amend. II.

119 Rick Lynch, "A Sure-Fire Argument on the Second Amendment," The Future of Freedom Foundation, February 18, 2008, https://www.fff.org/explore-freedom/article/surefire-argument-amendment/.

120 Debates in the Several State Conventions, vol. III, 355.

121 Lynch, "Sure-Fire Argument on the Second Amendment."

122 Lynch, "Sure-Fire Argument on the Second Amendment."

123 Lynch, "Sure-Fire Argument on the Second Amendment."

124 Federalist, no. 84 (Alexander Hamilton), 535.

125 Federalist, no. 6 (Alexander Hamilton), 34–35.

126 Federalist, no. 51 (James Madison), 325.

127 John Adams, The Works of John Adams, vol. VI (Boston: Charles C. Little and James Brown, 1851), 114.

128 Adams, Defence of the Constitutions, vol. III, 214–16, emphasis in original.

129 Adams, Defence of the Constitutions, vol. III, 363.

130 John Adams, A Defence of the Constitutions of Government of the United States of America, vol. IV (Boston: Edmund Freeman, 1788), 103.

131 Edward McNall Burns, James Madison: Philosopher of the Constitution (Octagon Books, 1968), 30.

132 Samuel Adams to Samuel Cooper, April 30, 1776, in The Writings of Samuel Adams, vol. III, ed. Harry Alonzo Cushing (G. P. Putnam's Sons, 1907), 284.

133 The Debates in the Several State Conventions, on the Adoption of the Federal Constitution, as Recommended by the General Convention at Philadelphia, in 1787, vol. I, ed. Jonathan Elliot (New York: Burt Franklin, 1888), 438–39.
134 Federalist, no. 34 (Alexander Hamilton), 200.
135 Federalist, no. 6 (Alexander Hamilton), 32–34.
136 Thomas Jefferson, "Kentucky Resolutions of 1798 [Jefferson's Draft]," in The Papers of Thomas Jefferson: 1 January 1798–31 January 1799, vol. 30, ed. Barbara B. Oberg (Princeton University Press, 2003), 536–43.
137 Federalist, no. 37 (James Madison), 225.
138 Adams, Defence of the Constitutions, vol. III, 215–16.
139 Adams, Defence of the Constitutions, vol. III, 217.
140 Adams, Defence of the Constitutions, vol. III, 283.
141 Federalist, no. 15 (Alexander Hamilton), 94.
142 David Hume, "Of the Independency of Parliament," in Essays and Treatises on Several Subjects (London: A. Millar, 1760), 75.
143 Federalist, no. 10 (James Madison), 61, emphasis added.
144 Federalist, no. 15 (Alexander Hamilton), 94.
145 Federalist, no. 49 (James Madison), 317.
146 Madison, Papers, Purchased by Order of Congress, vol. II, 805.
147 Madison, Letters and Other Writings of James Madison, vol. IV, 22–23.
148 Adams, Defence of the Constitutions, vol. III, 271.
149 The Debates in the Several State Conventions on the Adoption of the Federal Constitution as Recommended by the General Convention at Philadelphia 1787 Together with the Journal of the Federal Convention, vol. III, ed. Jonathan Elliot (New York: Burt Franklin, 1787), 87.

150 Madison, Papers, Purchased by Order of Congress, vol. II, 805.
151 Adams, Defence of the Constitutions, vol. III, 216.
152 Adams, The Works of John Adams, vol. VI, 484.
153 Madison, Papers, Purchased by Order of Congress, vol. II, 753.
154 Madison, Debates on the Adoption of the Federal Constitution, vol. V, 138.
155 Federalist, no. 10 (James Madison), 57–62.
156 John Adams to Mercy Otis Warren, July 30, 1807, Founders Online, National Archives, accessed March 11, 2025, https://founders.archives.gov/documents/Adams/99-02-02-5199.
157 John Adams, Autobiography of John Adams, in The Works of John Adams, vol. VI (Boston: Charles C. Little and James Brown, 1851), 508.
158 Journal and Debates of the Federal Convention, Held at Philadelphia, from May 14, to September 17, 1787, with the Constitution of the United States, vol. IV, ed. Jonathan Elliot (Washington: Printed by and for the Editor, 1830), 82.
159 Federalist, no. 6 (Alexander Hamilton), 34–35.
160 James Madison to Thomas Jefferson, October 17, 1788, in Tucker, Life of Thomas Jefferson, vol. I, 278.
161 Adams, Defence of the Constitutions, vol. III, 218.
162 John Adams to Thomas Jefferson, November 15, 1813, in The Writings of Thomas Jefferson: Being His Autobiography, Correspondence, Reports, Messages, Addresses, and Other Writings, Official and Private, Published by the Order of the Joint Committee of Congress on the Library, from the Original Manuscripts, vol. VI, ed. H. A. Washington (New York: John C. Riker, 1837), 254.
163 Federalist, no. 62 (James Madison), 388.

164 Federalist, no. 34 (Alexander Hamilton), 200.

165 James Madison to Thomas Jefferson, October 17, 1788, in Tucker, Life of Thomas Jefferson, vol. I, 278, emphasis in original.

166 Paper money?! Wow! Who saw that coming?

167 Madison, Papers, Purchased by Order of Congress, vol. II, 1142.

168 Those who would seek to make all of society "level," especially in the monetary sense by distributing property such that all would have an equal share.

169 Adams, The Works of John Adams, vol. VI, 118.

170 Federalist, no. 54 (James Madison), 344.

171 Federalist, no. 10 (James Madison), 61.

172 Marginal note in Adams's copy of "Thoughts on Government."

173 James Madison to Thomas Jefferson, October 17, 1788, in Tucker, Life of Thomas Jefferson, vol. I, 277–78.

174 Thomas Jefferson, The Writings of Thomas Jefferson: Being His Autobiography, Correspondence, Reports, Messages, Addresses. and Other Writings, Official and Private, Published by the Order of the Joint Committee of Congress of the Library, from the Original Manuscripts, vol. VIII, ed. H. A. Washington (Washington, DC: Taylor & Maury, 1854), 361, emphasis added.

175 Federalist, no. 62 (James Madison), 388.

176 Federalist, no. 63 (James Madison), 394.

177 John Adams, quoted in Joseph Story, Commentaries on the Constitution of the United States: With a Preliminary Review of the Constitutional History of the Colonies and States Before the Adoption of the Constitution (Boston: Little, Brown, and Company, 1878), 397–98.

178 John Adams, "Thoughts on Government," in The Works of John Adams, vol. IV (Boston: Charles C. Little and James Brown, 1851), 195.

179 Adams, "Opinions of Philosophers," in The Works of John Adams, vol. IV, 407.

180 Federalist, no. 70 (Alexander Hamilton), 440–41.

181 Federalist, no. 73 (Alexander Hamilton), 459.

182 Collier and Collier, Decision in Philadelphia, 53.

183 John Adams, "A Dissertation on the Canon and Feudal Law," in John Adams, The Political Writings of John Adams: Representative Selections, ed. George A. Peek Jr., (Bobbs-Merrill Educational Publishing, 1954), 13.

184 Thomas Jefferson, Memoir, Correspondence, and Miscellanies, from the Papers of Thomas Jefferson, vol. I, ed. Thomas Jefferson Randolph (Charlottesvile: F. Carr, and Co., 1829), 66.

185 Thomas Paine, Common Sense: Addressed to the Inhabitants of America (Philadelphia: J. Almon, 1776), 1.

186 Thomas Jefferson to James Madison, December 29, 1787, in Thomas Jefferson, Memoir, Correspondence, and Miscellanies, from the Papers of Thomas Jefferson, vol. II, ed. Thomas Jefferson Randolph (Charlottesvile: F. Carr, and Co., 1829), 276.

187 Thomas Jefferson to Colonel Carrington, May 27, 1788, in Thomas Jefferson, The Writings of Thomas Jefferson: Being His Autobiography, Correspondence, Reports, Messages, Addresses, and Other Writings, Official and Private, Published by the Order of the Joint Committee of Congress on the Library, from the Original Manuscripts, vol. II, ed. H. A. Washington (New York: John C. Riker, 1853), 404.

188 Adams, "A Dissertation on the Canon and Feudal Law," 13.
189 Jefferson, "Notes on the State of Virginia," in Writings of Thomas Jefferson, vol. VIII, 400.
190 Madison, "On Property," in Letters and Other Writings of James Madison, vol. IV, 478.
191 Federalist, no. 14 (James Madison), 84.
192 Federalist, no. 14 (James Madison), 84, emphasis added.
193 Federalist, no. 32 (Alexander Hamilton), 189, emphasis in original.
194 Federalist, no. 39 (James Madison), 241, emphasis in original.
195 Federalist, no. 40 (James Madison), 246–47.
196 Federalist, no. 45 (James Madison), 292.
197 Marbury v. Madison, 5 U.S. (1 Cranch) 137 (1803).
198 Marbury v. Madison, 5 U.S. (1 Cranch) 137.
199 Robert H. Bork, The Tempting of America: The Political Seduction of the Law (Simon & Schuster, 1991), 52, emphasis added.
200 Bork, Tempting of America, 52.
201 Federalism: created by the Enumeration.
202 Bork, Tempting of America, 53.
203 Bork, Tempting of America, 56.
204 Marbury, 5 U.S., quoted in Bork, Tempting of America, 24.
205 Bork, Tempting of America, 147, emphasis added.
206 Bork, Tempting of America, 153, emphasis added.
207 Bork, Tempting of America, 171, emphasis added.
208 Bork, Tempting of America, 31.
209 Bork, Tempting of America, 31.
210 Bork, Tempting of America, 153.
211 Bork, Tempting of America, 52.

212 Congress was empowered to ban the importation of slaves starting in 1808, but that was all.

213 Bork, Tempting of America, 184–85, emphasis added.

214 Federalist, no. 41 (James Madison), 259.

215 U.S. Const. preamble.

216 U.S. Const. art. I, § 8, cl. 18.

217 That pesky enumeration again!

218 James Madison to James Robertson, April 20, 1831, in Madison, Letters and Other Writings of James Madison, vol. IV, 171–72.

219 James Madison to Edmund Pendleton, January 21, 1792, in James Madison, Letters and Other Writings of James Madison, Fourth President of the United States, vol. I (Philadelphia: J. B. Lippincott & Co., 1867), 546, emphasis in original.

220 Thomas Jefferson to Albert Gallatin, June 16, 1817, in Thomas Jefferson, Thomas Jefferson: Letters and Addresses, ed. William B. Parker and Jonas Viles (Sun Dial Classics Co., 1908), 259.

221 Federalist, no. 41 (James Madison), 259.

222 Federalist, no. 41 (James Madison), 259–60.

223 Federalist, no. 33 (Alexander Hamilton), 193–94, emphasis in original, uppercase letters in original.

224 Federalist, no. 63 (James Madison), 394.

225 James McClellan, Liberty, Order, and Justice: An Introduction to the Constitutional Principles of American Government, 3rd ed. (Liberty Fund, 2000), 90.

226 Federalist, no. 63 (James Madison), 394.

227 Federalist, no. 63 (James Madison), 394.

www.ingramcontent.com/pod-product-compliance
Lightning Source LLC
LaVergne TN
LVHW090401210926
848480LV00002B/417